The Sausage Book

A book on all things Sausages

by

Paul Peacock

Published 2006

Copyright © Paul Peacock

ISBN 978-1-904871-17-0

A catalogue record for this book is available from
the British Library.

Published by
Farming Books and Videos Ltd.
PO Box 536
Preston
PR2 9ZY
www.farmingbooksandvideos.com

Cover design and drawings by Firecatcher Books.
Designed and set by Farming Books and Videos Ltd.

Printed and bound in Great Britain by
Cromwell Press.

This book is dedicated to
The Rt. Honourable Jim Hacker MP

who stopped the EU from
reclassifying the British Sausage
as the
'Emulsified, High-Fat, Offal Tube'
in BBC's 'Yes Minister!'

Contents

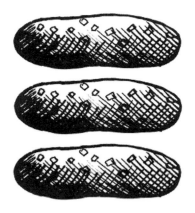

Introduction

This book is unashamedly about British sausages first and foremost, the kind you fry in a pan or grill or cook in a stew. Of course, there are recipes among these pages for dried, spiced and smoked sausages, chorizo, salamis and frankfurters But since the climate of the UK tends to render the making of uncooked, spiced, slicing sausage a slightly haphazard process, this guide concentrates, albeit not exclusively, on traditional British sausages.

We make no apology for this because British sausages are among the greatest, most versatile and exciting foodstuffs in the world.

Sausage making is enjoying a renaissance in modern times as more people demand better quality food. Of course, love them or loathe them, supermarkets have encouraged people to buy sausages from all around the world, and a bewildering variety have found their way into the daily diet of many people. It's not just the highly spiced products from hot countries which are being consumed in increasing numbers. Local, traditional sausages such as black pudding, haggis and county sausages too are selling once more in large numbers.

When I was a boy, a sausage was pink and moist and was fried in a pan, and very few people bought salami or chorizo. Today, however, sales of traditional sausages are being caught up by the dried variety and the growing smallholding movement has provided an impetus for turning home grown meat into sausages of all kinds.

Making sausages is actually very simple and once you get started you will not want to eat anyone else's. There has been, in recent years, an assault on sausages because of worries about their health status. All that fat and salt, quite rightly, caused the medical profession to raise their eyebrows about what we were eating. However, when you make your own sausages, you are in control of what goes into them. You can make low salt, no salt, healthy low fat, or even polyunsaturated beneficial fat sausages if you wish. Of course, you can also make unhealthy sausages too! It's entirely up to you.

Perhaps most exciting of all are the numbers of recipes for gourmet sausages. Flavoured with fruits, exotic spices and various meats, even vegetarian, you can virtually make a meal in a skin if you like. There is even a recipe for an egg, bacon and sausage sausage somewhere out there!

Perhaps the best reason of all to make your own sausages is because it is great fun. I hope, like me, you will end up spending many hours in the kitchen simply laughing as you fill your yard of casing. Indeed, the more rudimentary your equipment the funnier the process.

Whether you are buying this book to make your own sausages, or you intend to sell your produce at farmers' markets or country fairs, you will find both the techniques and the recipes to make dozens of sausages from all over the world, as well as a list of suppliers of casings, spices and equipment.

Happy Stuffing!

Paul Peacock
Manchester 2006

1 Chapter One
History in a Skin

Along with dogs, pigs are the oldest domesticated animals on earth. They have been kept for well over 10,000 years, first in Sumaria, now Iraq, and then out through Asia into China. There is plenty of evidence that mankind was making pork sausages as long as 9000 years ago.

The sausage needed two inventions to evolve. Careful butchery and the curing or preserving of meat with salt and other spices began in Babylonia and China. Good utensils, sharp knives which could be re-sharpened and the ability to resource vast amounts of water to clean out the intestines all combined to make the sausage a possibility.

The first written evidence of recipes we have for sausages come from 3000 BC in Sumeria. It is probable that we have been making sausages for much longer than we have been able to write, the recipes being passed down through the ages as tales and stories. Indeed, some scholars even believe that writing itself was developed to enable people to remember recipes.

Largely due to climate, sausages of a certain type have been made in the same locality and have become part of their respective culture. Some popular sausage types are probably many thousands of years old and possibly predate even recorded history. The sausage is a link to the past that is still popular today. History in a skin.

The dried and spiced sausages of North Africa that are uncooked and preserved with salt are as much a consequence of their locality and its prevailing weather as is the wet sausage of more northern, temperate climates.

The modern word for sausage comes from the Latin salsus; to salt. But there are a number of alternative names, some of which could have quite a different origin. For example, the French boudin is translated into English as 'pudding'. Boudin noir is black pudding, which we all know to be a fat, spiced, blood sausage and not a sweet pudding at all. The Haggis was described by Burns as "The Chieftain of the Pudding Race" and refers to the fact that the word pudding is old English for boiled sausage. But then some scribes believe that the word boudin comes from the Celtic word bod, which is translated penis, so then boudin could, therefore, be a little penis!

The Greeks loved sausage, as did the Romans. They were written about by the former and spread around the known world by the latter. In particular Roman sausages, often a combination of pig meat, cereals, blood, herbs and fish sauce, were used in religious festivals associated with fertility. These festivals frequently ended in orgies and when the Emperor Constantine converted to Christianity, sausages were described as sinful and outlawed for the next 600 years. Despite this, the popularity of the sausage remained unabashed, and even in Rome was still consumed with gusto.

By the tenth century sausages were more or less set as standard cullinary forms in each European region. The hot countries of the south had long developed dried sausages, highly spiced and ready to eat. The salamis and chorizos of Portugal, Spain and Italy were preserved by salt and drying and could last for a year. The recipes for these sausages were carried around Europe by founding Abbots as the monastic version of Catholicism spread north from its powerhouse in Italy and Spain.

Where the climate proved unsuitable for curing dried sausages, which tended to rot away in a humid atmosphere, alternatives were developed. Smoked cured sausage which remained wet and would last only a few days at best, replaced dried sausage in the wetter north.

By the time of the Norman Conquest in 1066, the commonplace sausages of Europe had become standard cuisine. In England chitterlings, a mixture of pork, fat and sage, resembled the common banger in shape, casing and size only. What we now recognise as sausage meat would have been unheard of in the middle ages with hardly any cereal being used in their manufacture, only meat, albeit often the poorest quality cuts and offal. The cost of feeding a pig to get it to its killing weight was expensive;

not a bit of it was to be wasted. Sausages became a way of preserving the less appetising cuts of meat which simply could not be thrown away.

There are very few traditional recipes for small game sausages in the UK because the rights of peasants to take pigeon and rabbit from common land was established in the Magna Carta in 1215. Consequently there was no need to preserve small game in sausages; this type of meat was always fresh and reasonably plentiful. You could always go and trap another rabbit, but a pig, with over a hundred pounds of useable meat, took a lot of preserving. So in the UK we came to eat more basic pork sausages than any other kind.

Sausages are mentioned in a fourteenth century source known as *Le Ménagier de Paris*. This is a set of instructions from a very wealthy sixty year old husband to his fifteen year old wife, written sometime in 1392.

"When you have killed your pig, take the flesh of the ribs and the best fat, as much of the one as of the other, in such quantity as you would make sausages; and cause it to be minced and hashed up very small by a pastry cook."

Of course, fat itself is a very effective preservative, hence he didn't refer to salt.

Sausages were mostly absent from cook books of the period. Instructions were given in such terms as "wash out the skins in the usual way" or "pound the meat as you would for sausages". It was simply assumed that one of the basic prerequisites for cooking would include the skills required for making sausages. It seems that, even after many thousands of years, cooking was still communicated largely by word of mouth.

Sausages were not linked together until the time of Charles I, who was said to enjoy them very much, as did Queen Victoria and George V. The old Queen's sausage was not ground at all, but chopped and stuffed into casings by hand.

Almost every county of the UK has its own type of sausage, mostly based on which spices grow well in the area, or because of the culture of the locality. For example, South Lancashire is famous for blood sausages largely because the pork meat was destined to be eaten elsewhere. Lincolnshire sausage was packed with sage and Cumberland sausage was heavy on pepper where it came ashore at Whitehaven.

Sausage meat is a relatively new idea. It is interesting to see that some recipes call for 'good quality sausage meat.' It is a mixture of minced pork and rusk, and frequently contains various quantities of water. The word 'banger' became popular because wartime sausages contained so much water that the steam would split the skins in an explosive attempt to escape. To stop the sausages becoming an exploded mess in the pan they were pricked with a fork before frying. However, home made sausages need not be pricked at all because their water content should be low and the fat content adds much to the flavour, so you do not want it to escape into the pan.

Home made sausages are more popular than ever as people find themselves more discerning about the quality of their food. For comparatively little effort and with almost no equipment, you can enjoy the highest quality food made to your own specification. You can make sausages that everyone in the family can enjoy, spicy or plain – even vegetarian. Of course, celebrity chefs all over the country have introduced the sausage to high class, and high paying, gastronomic fayre. Almost every restaurant includes them on the menu and the sausage is currently enjoying speciality status as evidenced by the salmon and caviar sausages on one London menu.

$\textstyle{2}$ Chapter Two
Getting Started

Sausage making is comparable, as a skill, to most jobs in the kitchen. If you can bake bread or make a pie then you will most likely be able to make your own sausages. These chapters are for those new to sausage making. Later in the book we will add a few notes for those planning to go into commercial sausage manufacturing in a small way, from either a smallholding or farm shop. That section will contain all the information required to meet the relevant laws and conditions for such a venture.

Equipment

Most kitchens already have most of the items needed to make sausages. It doesn't take a lot and you can make do with almost nothing. Most equipment on sale for sausage making is purely for convenience. You can stuff sausages by hand and you can grind your meat on a slab with a big pebble, as they used to do centuries ago, but you probably wouldn't want to.

Scales

Scales are important and you may wish to invest in two sets; one for measuring kilos of meat or fat, and another for weighing out grams of ingredients such as salt. If you are going to make commercial dried sausages you need to be able to measure critical but small quantities of essential preservative.

One thing to remember is that many recipes call for percentages by weight, not volume. In the case of water, a kilo occupies exactly one litre, so you can use a measuring jug, but if you are adding something like olive oil, this is lighter and will need to be weighed out unless the recipe states a fluid measure. You will have to bear this in mind if you invent your own sausages.

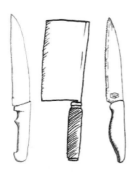

Knives

A really sharp knife is important. Say, for example, you do not like the skin on belly pork, then you will need to cut it off, and this is extremely hard work with a blunt knife. A good boning knife is an absolute must if you intend to take meat off the bone. My own butcher, a Rick Stein Food Hero, buys four pigs a week and uses the shoulder to make sausages, the meat pared from the bone with a deadly sharp knife.

Perhaps more important than the knife is a stone to keep it sharp and the ability to use it.

Grinders

You can still buy, very cheaply, a hand made grinder like you used to find in a butcher's shop or on grandmother's kitchen table. You can get new ones from various UK distributors, mostly manufactured in Europe.

These machines have grinding plates inside them and discs with holes which tear the meat to a paste as it is forced through by the Archimedes screw that is in turn cranked by the handle. You can grind your meat a number of times to create various consistencies and then remove the discs altogether to use the same machine to stuff your casings. The discs represent fine, medium and rough grinds.

These machines are dismantled easily for cleaning, and for comparatively little expense they will last a lifetime. You can buy plastic ones that do the job but I worry about their long term use.

A number of different electrical grinders/stuffers are available at various prices and standards. I always think it is most efficient to buy the best machine that you can afford so if you cannot get a high quality electrical grinder/stuffer, a really high quality mechanical one is a better buy.

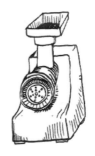

Considering a new grinder?

When first using the old type hand cranked grinder, the product will probably be covered in a thin film of mineral oil which is easily washed off. However, the inside of the machine will be similarly protected. Buy some fat, pork fat will do, and when you have cleaned the outside, grind the fat through the machine until all the black comes out and the fat is aroma free.

When you have used your grinder give it a good spray with a general kitchen disinfectant before washing it in very hot water.

If you have your own meat to make sausages, or turn over a large quantity, more than 5 Kilos, then a powerful grinder is needed. The more meat you have, the more powerful the motor needs to be to avoid putting it under too much strain. Look for grinders that are 'over engineered' with good quality metal pieces, and most importantly, a clamp to secure it to the work bench; preferably with at least a pair of really good quality 'G-clamps.'

Food Processor

A food processor does chop up meat but tends to liquidise rather than grind, so the judicious use of the pulse button allows for a mixture which is part paste, part fine pieces and part coarser pieces. Food processors are fine for the small kitchen where comparatively small quantities of meat are being processed.

Stuffers

If you do not use a grinder to make your mix, you will need a stuffer of some kind.

You don't need to stuff your sausage mix into a skin, animal or otherwise! Skinless sausages can be made by simply rolling your mixture into appropriate shapes. You can also buy caul, which is the fatty membrane that connects all the organs in the body. You can wrap your sausages in it, and since it is mostly fat, the cooked sausage is very succulent.

Piping bag

Greek, Roman and Medieval sausage makers did not have a lot of equipment, just a sharp knife and a lot of intestines. You can use a piping bag to stuff casings and it works quite well too! If you are going to do this with a piping bag you must remember to fit a long nozzle and make your mixture pastier than normal. I have found that double the amount of water makes the bag easier to squeeze. You will certainly end up with a reputation for having a good strong handshake!

Funnel

You can buy a sausage funnel, which is slightly easier to use and resembles a kitchen funnel except it does not taper. This is important because otherwise everything gets stuck in the tapered tube. A piece of dowelling that just fits in the tube of the funnel can be used to flush the mixture into the skin, almost a sausage length at a time.

Mechanical stuffer

For commercial use vertical stuffers which take around 20 kilos of material at a time are ideal.

There are three important considerations on buying a stuffer. It must be easy to clean and present no kinks or hiding place for meat to accumulate. It must fasten to the work bench effectively and it must allow you to produce a decent amount of sausage without having to stop and reload every few minutes. Once you have managed the trick, and it's a very easy trick to manage, you will realise that stuffing sausages is a rhythmic process.

Although you wouldn't think it, manual stuffers allow you to gauge the exact pressure needed to cause the mixture to fill the casing at a constant rate. Large capacity barrel type stuffers that have a disc attached to a heavy duty screw will allow for up to 10 kilos of mixture to be delivered steadily at a time. The efficient use of this type of machine frequently demands more than one pair of hands. Electrical stuffers can be used single handed much more easily, but push out mix at a rate that can take some getting used to. Industrial electrical stuffers have a knee switch. You can turn the machine on and off and still have both hands free to handle the sausages.

Whichever type of stuffer you decide on, you need a minimum of three nozzles, a small one with a diameter around a centimetre, one around 1.5 cm and one around 2 cm. The wider the nozzle the thicker the sausage and the easier the mixture exudes from the machine.

Trays and bowls

This might seem silly but the best thing in the kitchen for making sausages is a tray. Trying to catch them into a bowl or a plate simply will not do. An easy clean steel tray, preferably two or three of them if you make large batches of sausages, is ideal. You will also need a large mixing bowl, preferably steel, to take the heat away from the meat.

Sausage making is a little like making pastry in that cool hands and cool equipment is best so choose equipment that transmits heat away from the sausage.

Thermometer

When you cook sausages (and you will see that we recommend you also cook all your dried and spicy sausage) you will need to make sure that the centre reaches at least 75° Celsius and remains so for at least twenty minutes.

Kitchen thermometers with a bimetallic strip probe are the best, but you can get electronic ones. The idea is to plunge the probe into the sausage and hold it until the temperature stops rising.

Of course, everyone simply cooks their ordinary, everyday, traditional sausages in a pan and instinctively knows when they are cooked. The thermometer, however, is very useful for checking the core temperature

of dried sausages that are cooked before hanging.

Smokers

Hot smokers both cook your sausage and smoke the food at the same time. They are not just built for sausages, but can be used to cook any foods. They can be used to cook and smoke dried sausages for subsequent hanging and they can also be used as a steamer, with no wood, to simply cook.

They consist of a metal tin, about twice the size of a large pan with a tray system inside to separate the wood from the food, but allowing the smoke to pervade the whole. There is also a sealed lid which stops most of the smoke escaping.

You place chippings inside the base of the smoker and place it on the heat. The whole container becomes hot and consequently both cooks and smokes the contents simultaneously.

Cold smokers

There are plans available for making cold smokers which consist of a fire and a tube to a separate container where the food is hung to be smoked. Some old houses also have chimney spaces for smoking. However, if you are serious about smoking sausages you will probably wish to buy a  smoking cabinet which does the job in a professional way.

They are not cheap, but are the state of the art, stainless steel, easy clean, option.

Dehumidifiers

If you are short of a place to hang your sausage you can use a dehumidifier to do the same job. These pull water from the atmosphere and consequently any food that is in the container. They come in various forms; plastic home use machines and more substantial (and expensive) commercial ones.

Vacuum pack

Well, you don't really need it to make sausages, but vacuum packing is quite cheap; a birthday present for someone who has everything! The sausages thus sealed have an extended shelf life, around 50% longer if kept at appropriate temperatures, and they are not tainted by anything else around them. The skins remain untroubled by oxidation from the atmosphere, and the product seems to be fresher when cooked.

For those of you who have your own animals with which to make sausages a good trick is to store the meat in vacuum packs and frozen ready for a sausage making session. It is one of those little extravagances that can be justified if you have a good imagination. Wet sausages are hardly ever sold in vacuum packs, but dried ones frequently are.

What Should You Expect?

Sausages are not pink! Pigs are certainly not all pink so why should sausages be pink. It is well known in the sausage industry that people buy food with their eyes and not their taste buds. Saddleback pigs are black and white, Tamworths are grey, Oxford Sandy and Blacks are just that; sandy and black, Welsh pigs are black, Gloucester Old Spots are black and human flesh coloured, Welsh Whites are, er, white; SO WHY SHOULD SAUGAGES BE PINK?

Pork isn't pink, but bacon is pink because the chemical saltpetre is added to make it pink and not the more natural grey. On the shelves in the supermarkets people only buy pink sausages, but now you have the opportunity to control what goes into your food. Saltpetre adds nothing at all to your sausage in terms of flavour. Similarly, when it is found in bacon, all this chemical does is hold the colour; bacon without saltpetre added is grey in colour. It's actually called green bacon, tastes just as good and is just as well preserved.

Start Small and Get Stuck In

Try around a kilo of meat as an experiment. Pork shoulder would be ideal. (See the chapter 'Basic Sausage Making') Then get your hands dirty, if you will forgive the tautology there! If you were to use belly you might find the skin a little difficult to deal with, and since shoulder is much like belly without the skin, you might as well use it. If you buy your meat from a real butcher, you could ask him to grind it for you.

If you ask nicely, he will probably also provide you with some skins and rusk, so your first experience of sausage making need not be that messy and may even be quite inexpensive.

There are many recipes for sausage making that involve sequential refrigeration at various stages, popping the meat in to cool before grinding, mixing and then cooling again to allow the flavours to gel together, or waiting for this and that to happen. But for most recipes JUST GET ON WITH IT! Be confident with your measurements, then grind, mix and stuff those casings.

Economics – Is it Really Worth It?

Having bought a hand grinding machine for over thirty pounds and spent money on skins and spices and a pile of meat, and then taken a whole afternoon to make your sausages you may find yourself asking if it was really worth it?

The answer should be a resounding Yes. You will never produce sausages as inexpensively as the cheap ones that you can find in any supermarket. But these will be nothing like your own. Supermarket sausages are around 40% meat content and taste nothing like sausages which have almost double that amount of meat in them – and decent meat at that! New rules will bemuse you with what they can classify as meat these days. Thankfully they are not allowed to include high pressure reclaimed meat in their allocation, but a 40% meat sausage might contain precious little of what you would recognise as actual meat.

To buy a sausage that is 80% meat, real meat that walked around, low salt, no monosodium glutamate, no colours or flavourings, will cost you at least three times as much as your first home made batch.

Why Make Your Own Sausages?

There are some other excellent reasons for making your own sausages. You make them with your own ingredients, in your own kitchen. Pride is probably the best seasoning any food can ever have.

Sausages have been the ultimate convenience food for millennia. More than just a way of preserving meat, the casing makes them easy to cook and simple to serve. Once cooked they can travel anywhere and be eaten cold in a picnic, at work, in a field or in the office.

Most fast food outlets sell sausages. They are a staple, even though they are now produced just as sausages in their own right and no longer for the two reasons for which they became popular in the first place, namely the need to preserve excesses of meat and as a way of making the least appetising cuts of meat palatable.

Making your own sausages is important for many reasons, some of which we will come back to time and again in this book.

They are still a convenience food, even though you may have gone to the effort of making them yourself. If you make sausages in batches and freeze them, or make dried sausages and use them ad hoc in the kitchen, they are still convenient. Of course you have gone to the trouble of batching them up, but this is simply a fun way of spending an afternoon – well it is in our kitchen. With plenty in the freezer it is as easy as buying them from the supermarket.

You can make a lot of sausages, particularly if you have your own meat or can buy in bulk. You have the opportunity to make the best of surpluses; particularly knowing the origin of your own produce you can make the very best. There is a skill to making sausages, but no more than is needed to make an average family meal.

It is possible to make sausages that are tailor made to individual requirements, everything from full fat high flavour sausages, what we all know as bangers, fish bangers or vegetarian sausages. By the same rule it is possible to make a number of gourmet sausages, as flavoursome and exclusive as anything you will find anywhere.

You will know exactly what has gone into your own sausages. No chemicals, no additives, the best meat and top quality ingredients. More than anything you can determine the actual meat content of your own sausages, which will go a long way to making them special.

We live in a world where everything is done for profit. We will see in the history of the sausage that the knowledge needed to make this life saving food has been passed down for hundreds of generations, from a time before writing was even invented, let alone popular. Why, after such a long time, should such an important skill be lost to the world? By learning to make sausages you are keeping alive not only a tradition but a vital facet of human knowledge.

3 Chapter Three
Some Golden Rules

We all know that rules are there to be broken. Yet it is imperative that rules related to cleanliness are rigidly and consistently applied. To put it simply, the aim is not to kill yourself, or anyone else for that matter.

Not to put too fine a point on it, a sausage is a banquet for bacteria, and they will double in number every twenty minutes. A single bacterium will, after eight hours, have multiplied to over 16 million individuals. This is fine for the vast majority of bacteria which form an important part of many foods, but for a handful of poisonous ones the results of ingesting them can be catastrophic.

In Order to Avoid Them...

Be scrupulously clean at all times

Disinfect everything
Use utensils that are easy to clean
Wash your hands – often
Use ultra fresh materials
Store spices correctly
Cook everything properly

The disease known as Botulism was first encountered in 1735 when a dozen people tucked into a meal of German sausages and all died. Botulism literally means sausage disease. It is caused by a bacterium which lives quite happily in soil but under certain conditions, in large enough numbers, gives off a chemical which is lethal to humans.

The single most important factor to remember when making sausages is cleanliness. Contamination from objects in the kitchen, our clothes, our skin, hair, spittle, nose and other places that shall be kept from this book, should be kept to an absolute minimum.

You cannot be too fanatical about keeping everything clean. Everything must be disinfected and, as far as possible, free from contaminants. The worktops should be disinfected before and after making sausages, and sometimes between stages in the process. Utensils and receptacles must be scrupulously clean and sterilised – washed in hot soapy water and then rinsed for a long time in boiling water.

There are two basic ways of ensuring that bacteria do not spoil your food, which work in tandem: stopping bacteria, as far as is possible, from getting onto your food in the first place and keeping them from multiplying on your food when they do get on it.

It is worth noting that it is not the bacteria themselves that kill. It is their waste products known as toxins that do the most harm. You can kill the bacterium but its toxins will remain and if there is sufficient then symptoms will follow.

A part of keeping food fresh is reducing the total number of bacteria, and thus reducing the concentration of toxin in the food.

Cooling and Freezing

Bacteria reproduce more slowly as the temperature falls but they are rarely killed outright, even when the food is frozen solid. In such circumstances the freezing bacteria form spores, thousands of them, ready to burst into life as the food warms up again. This is why you cannot refreeze food, since you will be turning thousands of spores into reproducing bacteria.

Cooling to lower than 4° Celsius will inhibit the growth of most bacteria so instead of multiplying by a factor of thousands they only double in number in the course of a few hours. This is enough to keep the food fresh for up to three days.

Freezing food completely will stop bacterial growth. Assuming the food was very fresh when it was prepared there should be a limited bacterial population and the food will last a considerable time in a frozen condition.

Another reason for freezing pork is to combat the remote possibility of contracting triconosis. This is caused by a parasite and can be found in the UK on rare occasions. The meat should be frozen to -20° Celsius for a month. However the larvae are killed by heating above 75° Celsius for ten minutes. In the UK this problem only really occurs in meat that has been imported.

Isolation

Removing bacteria from the area where your sausages are kept is not so easy. Everything should be cleaned and disinfected. A favourite disinfectant is Milton, which leaves little or no taint and kills bacteria completely.

It is important to remember that most bacteria originate in soil, so wash your hands, clean your finger nails, wear plastic gloves and maintain a high level of personal cleanliness. Always wear protective clothing – clean aprons and something to keep your hair out of the way.

Cover food with fresh cling film or foil before putting it into the fridge. Isolating your food from spoiling bacteria includes sterilising your implements and worktops. Just pouring boiling water over them is not enough – some spores can withstand boiling water for a few minutes.

Ingredients

Always wash your meat and other washable ingredients and make sure they are as fresh as possible. There are three methods of killing bacteria in food. Heat, osmotic disruption (which means forcing the water out of cells, both living or dead, by using either salt or sugar or drying), and chemicals which either attack bacteria directly or by making the food more acidic.

Heat

Most bacteria are killed by heating above 75° Celsius for ten minutes. A cooked sausage that is then vacuum packed will have a long shelf life, assuming it was free from bacteria in the actual packing process.

It is important to realise that a sausage which has been kept at room temperature for a week, and does not contain any form of preservative, including salt, will be packed with bacteria and, even if cooked, could be a threat to continued good health. Cooking does not remove the toxin, just the bacteria.

Heating your food to 75° Celsius for ten minutes should be enough to the ensure the safety of fresh food.

If you are contemplating producing dried sausage you might consider that it is best to cook them before hanging. It might not be authentic, but it is safe. You can cook uncooked sausages in a bain marie in the oven at 175° Celsius. Use a probe thermometer to check the internal temperature of the sausage.

Osmotic Disruption

This is a big title for a simple yet profound process. Water molecules are one of the smallest things in nature. They move around very quickly and more than anything else, water will permeate everything it comes into contact with. At the microscopic level, water will dilute strong concentrations of chemicals, even if it means this water has its origins inside a living cell. It is thus possible to drag the water from a bacterium by force, thus killing it, by simply placing a strong concentration of salt next to it.

Any bacterium is powerless to stop water from being pulled out of its cells if there happens to be a crystal of salt or sugar nearby. The consequence of this is that the cells are ruptured and the bacterium dies. So the addition of salt or sugar to food preserves it by osmotic disruption. Quite small concentrations of salt are enough to prolong the keeping qualities of food.

Drying the food and the addition of spices also has the same effect. The food is preserved because the bacteria are all dead. The only problem with drying is that it is not always possible to ensure that the very centre of the sausage has become dry enough to inhibit bacterial growth. For this reason, commercial dried sausage has to have other preservatives to ensure a safe product. This usually means saltpetre.

Chemical Action

Bacteria are killed by many natural substances – garlic juice, cayenne pepper and other preservatives, mainly nitrates and nitrites, which act directly on the bacterium. Substances that increase the acidity of the mixture also inhibit bacteria, so it is not unlikely to find ascorbic acid in bought sausages, along with sodium ascorbate as a buffer to keep the acidity up.

Follow the Recipes Before You Experiment

It really is easy to miscalculate, add too much salt, not enough fat, and make a sausage that is not very appetising. The sausage is quite complicated as a foodstuff and the constituent parts are there for a purpose. You might vary the ingredients, miss things out altogether, and any changes will have an effect on the final product that will most usually reveal itself in the cooking.

Keep it Simple

A sausage is essentially meat and salt and pepper. You do not have to add lots of flavours to it because the meat is flavoursome enough. When you add herbs make sure that they are rarely more than 2 – 3 % of the final mixture and do not make flavours compete in the sausage.

Casing

This is clearly there to hold the sausage together, but it does more. The contents are under slight pressure inside the skin, and this helps the cooking. As the skin cooks it shrinks, improving the shape of the sausage and compressing the contents still further. When the fat in the mixture melts it is forced into the whole of the stuffing under this pressure. Home made skinless sausages have a tendency to fall apart and can over cook at the open edges.

Always use the correct nozzle size for the skin you are about to stuff. Overstretching a skin over a nozzle will rip it and a loose skin will not fill properly.

A final consideration is that the skin holds the flavour into the sausage. For this reason they should not be pricked. Wartime sausages which contained a lot of water, would explode in the pan as the steam tried to escape. These sausages were pricked, but there is no need to do this with the homemade variety.

Fat

Fat is there for many reasons and, of course, many people now prefer a low fat diet for health reasons. One of the reasons for adding fat is cheapness. Lean meat is dearer than its fatty counterpart. Another reason is flavour. Fat acts as a solvent for all kinds of flavours that appear in the cooking process. To my mind a fatty sausage is more appetising than a lean one, but it cannot be denied that too much fat is harmful.

Another reason for fat is that it heats up and melts during the cooking process thus distributing heat evenly inside the sausage and cooking it from within. Low fat sausages are trickier to cook because the contents are very insulating. The outside cooks more quickly than the inside.

Water

This is a vital ingredient in a sausage. It helps the mixture become pliable and thus it will stuff more easily. Sausages are succulent and much of this comes from the added water whose content may, on occasion, exceed 10%.

Do not disparage the water content of homemade sausages. It is not there for cheapness. Without it the casings would be all but impossible to stuff.

Salt

This and other preserving chemicals are important if you want to keep sausages for more than a couple of days.

Low salt sausages are undoubtedly healthier, and the change in flavour from high salt to low salt is so easy to get used to that you do not notice it after a while.

No salt sausages will last a maximum of three days in the refrigerator, ordinary salt ones will be good for twice this.

Do not make a sausage with a salt content higher than 3% of its total weight.

Rusk or Breadcrumbs

We mention this elsewhere in this book but it is worth repeating. Rusk, breadcrumbs or cereal are an important part of a sausage. They bind the ingredients, soak up cooking juices and help improve the consistency. They add nothing to the flavour save in two very special sausages. Haggis and black pudding have a high cereal, content but no one would doubt they have their own very special flavour.

Ideally up to 15% of the sausage's weight could be cereal. In order to make a gluten free sausage you can replace the rusk with rice, nuts or soya products.

How to Make Breadcrumbs

Certain recipes call for dried breadcrumbs and others call for fresh. These are essentially the same and easily made in a food processor. Dried breadcrumbs are made by drying the bread in the oven at 75° Celsius. You can leave the oven door open if you like – pretend you are making a meringue. Fresh breadcrumbs are made by simply whizzing stale bread in the processor.

If you do not have a food processor you can dry your bread as above and then use a grater to create the crumbs. When the bread goes red you have cut your fingers!

Storage

Uncooked sausages should be sealed in an airtight container and can be kept for up to six days in the refrigerator. They can be frozen for three months. Before storage in any form, dry them off with either a clean paper towel or leave them to dry in the air. This will keep them from sticking together. If possible home made sausages should be stored singly and not knotted together. The links should be cut, so you have individuals. This is solely to keep air circulating around the product, and stop the accumulation of germs on moist surfaces.

Cooking

Sausages need careful cooking. It might seem that everyone knows how to cook sausages but remember, you are in effect cooking a cut of meat. Stuffing containing a lot of shoulder or belly pork needs slower cooking than a lot of lean meat.

Cook the un-pricked sausages on a medium heat and look through the skin to see the fat boiling inside. If your sausage is particularly thick, you might wish to check the internal temperature with a meat thermometer.

Sausages that are boiled generally rise to the surface when they are ready, and it is worth noting that water transmits heat much more efficiently than air
.

Although it is quick, I would not recommend cooking home made sausages in the microwave. They almost always become tough.

Home made sausages make the very best casseroles you can imagine. Special sausages with a higher meat and lower cereal content for casseroling, such as the Toulouse, are fantastic in an onion sauce.

4 Chapter Four
A Word About Casings

Sausages are stuffed into skins, also known as casings. It will come as no surprise that these skins originally come from the intestines of food animals, and although synthetic ones are available, natural casings are still the most popular.

Natural casings are made from sheep, cattle or pigs and come in various sizes. Traditionally pig or hog casings as they are called, come in two sizes, one from the large intestine and one from the small.

They are usually prepared in factories, although skins were once made in many butchers' shops, the contents being forced out with the back of a knife and then repeatedly washed, both inside and out.

Once cleaned, sausage skins are washed in brine and packed in salt. They are packaged in hanks, or bundles, tied up with a string and are around 20 metres long. They are vacuum packed in salt – usually brine that is so strong that the salt crystallises inside the package.

The casings are usually tailor made for certain recipes of which the most common is pork. Beef casings are frequently used for dried, semi-dried or spiced sausages.

All casings have to be subject to a microbial test which is administered by the European Natural Sausage Casing Association. (ENSCA). This now applies to any sausage or skins brought into any European market from countries outside Europe, where food health guidelines and regulations may not be as stringent.

Beef Casings

These are for dried, fermented and boiled sausages that need thick skins. The gut of a cow is so varied that there are many sized beef casings available, each having their own name depending which part of the world they came from.

Bungs are up to two feet long with a diameter of several inches are for large sausages, salami and black pudding.
Bladders are even larger and are used for slicing sausages like Mortadella.
Middles are from two inches wide and are the normal dried sausage casing. They can be boiled or dried to make spicy sausages, and they can be sewn together to make larger ones.
Rounds are an inch to two inches and are used for salami, black pudding and liverwurst.

Hog or Pig Casings

Much smaller and more delicate than beef, hog casings are the most commonly used partly because of their size and also for the texture of the skin once it is cooked.

Bungs are around an inch in diameter. I have used them to make Cumberland sausages, but they are equally at home being used for thin salami.
Middles sometimes known as chitterlings, are the general sausage skins. They can vary in size, are usually less than an inch, and are used for everything from breakfast sausage to long thin salami.

Sheep Casings

These are ideal for most sausages that you fry in a pan. They look small and thin but are quite strong and their texture once cooked is the best of all, in my opinion! They are around half to three quarters of an inch and are ideal for most 'British banger' type sausages.

Man-made Casings

These are available in a bewildering array of materials, shapes and sizes, from huge stomach like casings to ordinary sausage sized ones. You can even get vegetarian sausage casings.

Collagen

These casings are made from animal protein, usually from cattle. It is made from the under skin of the animal and then formed into a tube. They are exceptionally uniform in size and are used to make commercial sausages. They are best stuffed by a machine because once split, the whole batch can be ruined.

Fibrous

These are strengthened skins used for making dry, smoked and cured sausages. They are difficult to knot and have to be tied up because the skin will not grip the contents so well. They shrink on drying, tightening the sausage.

Synthetic

These are largely made from plastic and cannot be smoked as the plastic they are made from will be tainted, or will not allow the smoke through. The covering on smoked cheese, which is applied after smoking, is a good example of this material.

Using Casings (hold your nose!)

Your first job in making sausages is to soak the skins. By the time you have completed the other preparations the skins will be almost ready.

There is no other way of putting it; some casings smell, especially the sheep ones. The salt must be washed off the whole batch of casings, which will be attached to a piece of string. You are not only washing out the salt but the smell, which is quite strong. It does not mean that the skin is bad or off, they simply smell like that! They need to be washed inside and out. They are quite tough and you can handle them fairly easily.

You need to soak them in many changes of water for around half an hour (though hog casings will take a lot longer – an hour or two) and then give them a final rinse inside and out. The ends of the casing are attached to the string and if you lift it, the bundle of casings will fall over each other and look as though they are about to knot, but they rarely do. Simply tease the casing from the string.

The casings can knot if they are dry – sheep casings have a tendency to do this. Leave them in water and they tend to fall apart more easily.

You can find the opening of the casing with your thumb and charge the filling tube with the moist casing. Once you get used to this you can fill the 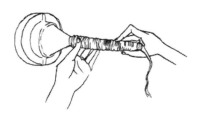 nozzle with a number of skins ready for continuous filling. Leave an inch or two over the nozzle end and do not knot the casing, Let the air pass through the nozzle and out of the untied end. Eventually, sausage mix will appear, dragging the casing off the nozzle.

Any casing you do not need can be covered in salt again and placed in the fridge in a plastic container. In this way there is absolutely no waste. You may find the re-salted casings a little more difficult to use. For a start they tend to twist a little and are more difficult to separate. They can be more brittle and burst more easily, but on the whole, with care, they are completely re-usable.

How Much to Use

Of course the thickness of the casing will affect the way the sausage is stuffed and how much filling you use. However, as a general rule, if you allow a metre of casing for every 500g of stuffing you have used, you will not be all that far out. This will give you plenty of space for linking.

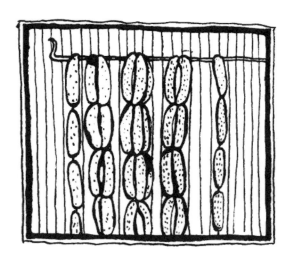

5 Chapter Five
How to Link Sausages

Everyone loves linked sausages, they look so good. The ability to do this sets you apart as a sausage producer, amateur or otherwise. In the UK sausages are generally linked into threes, and there are still competitions around the country to find the best.

Home made sausages are sometimes linked in twos for ease, but even this method has some secret methodologies.

It is best to do it when the skins are wet. If you are linking collagen casings then you should moisten them with cooking oil to make them more slippery.

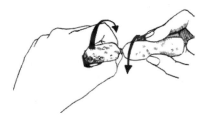

Making a single line of linked sausages

If you separate the contents of the sausage with the thumbs and fore fingers, you can then twist the sausage to make a link. Alternate the direction of twist with each link. This is the easiest way of making individual sausages. If you twist a good few times, the links can be cut to make individual sausages without fear of them undoing. The ends close up tightly as they dry out.

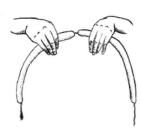

Linking in Twos

To make a double link leaving you with two sausages together, simply find the middle of the sausage and make a double length. At the apex, make a twist link, then twist the two strands of sausage over each other. Continue this along the length.

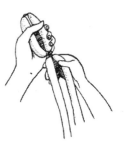

Linking in Threes

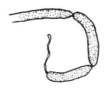

Make two links as though you were going to make single links. Make sure there is some skin hanging at the end of the sausage.

Tie this bit of skin to the end link of the second sausage. You now have a loop of sausage made of two links.

Now loop the rest of the sausage between the other two sausages.

When the sausage loop reaches the end of the first two, fold it round to create another loop through the end of the sausage.

Twist the topmost loop to make the link and repeat the process of looping and twisting until the whole sausage is used up.

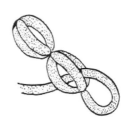

6 Chapter Six
Basic Sausage Making

Having gathered your equipment, whatever it might consist of, you are now ready to make your own sausages. If you expect to fall about laughing, or to create a final product that resembles a battlefield then you will be pleasantly surprised. The skills needed to create sausages are on a par with, though totally different from, cooking a Sunday roast. If you can do that, or learn how to do it, then you can make the very best sausages in the world.

This recipe is for a simple pork sausage which has nothing in it other than salt, pepper and a little cereal. You will need:

1 kilo of Pork Shoulder
200 g sausage making rusk, or breadcrumbs if you prefer
200 ml water

1 tsp salt
½ tsp pepper

1 mixing bowl
1 grinder or food processor
1 sausage stuffer
1.25 m sausage casing. Hog casings are easiest to use for first-timers
1 tray to collect the filling sausage
1 knife to cut the links

Clean and disinfect your work surfaces and utensils.

Open your packet of skins (never mind the smell) and place them in a bowl of clean water. Replace the water several times until the smell goes away. (I try to avoid running water at this stage because you can get smell laden splashes around the kitchen.)

Now rinse the skins under running water, both inside and out.

Lots of recipes call for the chilling of your meat, (See note in 'Some Golden Rules' about trichinosis) but for sausages that you are going to fry or grill or bake, you can just get stuck in.

Chop your meat into centimetre cubes and then grind them. If you have to use a food processor, pulse the machine to avoid it becoming like soup.

You can also add your other ingredients to this mix depending on the size of your food processor, otherwise, mix everything together in a large mixing bowl. This is the longest part of the operation and possibly the most important, particularly if you wish to keep your sausage for some time, or if you are making dried and spiced sausage.

It is important that you mix everything as thoroughly as you can. I tend to mix the dry ingredients together first, then mix this with the meat products. Another way of mixing is to add the smallest quantities to the water first and then use this to mix the stuffing.

Once you have created your sausage mix and are ready to stuff your casing, you can fry a small amount to check that you are happy with the seasoning.

Now find the end of your casing

This can be more fun than you may care for! Usually the casings are attached to a piece of string which, when you lift it out of the water, the casings attached to it fall under gravity like a dead alien. Moisten the delivery tube or nozzle of your stuffer and carefully push the casing on. You might imagine that you should tie the casing, but don't! Leave the end of the intestine open so that as you force the meat mixture through the air will escape. Once meat replaces air the skin will be pulled off the nozzle and into a collecting tray.

Starting to stuff the casings can be a daunting task, but is actually quite simple. You will benefit from an extra pair of hands, one to crank the machine (or start it working if it is electrical) and another to manage the flow of sausage from the other end.

The large capacity mechanical stuffers need quite a lot of effort to force the mixture down the nozzle, and sometimes this effort can dislodge the machine from the worktop. Make sure the attaching 'G-clamps' are very securely tightened.

You can control the thickness of the sausage by gently holding back the casing as it fills with mixture; this will allow more meat per centimetre of sausage, and consequently you get a thicker sausage.

Don't worry about breakages in the skin. It is bound to happen sometime in your career. Instead concentrate on maintaining a rhythm and an evenly filled sausage. The first few centimetres might be a little thinner than the rest. For your first try just let the meat take the casing without restriction. You do not need to over fill the casings; leave room for twisting your links.

If there are any air bubbles in the sausage you can prick them. Otherwise the casings will burst in the pan. You do not need to be microscopic in your inspection, only large air spaces need be dealt with. Alternatively, large bubbles can be cleverly incorporated into the twist link.

If you can, leave the sausages overnight to improve the flavour, and then cook them. Aficionados call this 'allowing the sausage to bloom.' I haven't managed this step yet. There is always a hot frying pan ready to receive the first few links.

Finally, clean down your equipment straight away, sterilising it all with boiling water if possible. This will make the next batch of sausages easier, though you will have to re-sterilise for each session.

Making Smoked Sausages

The basics for making dried and smoked sausages, the grinding and the stuffing, are very similar to those in wet sausages. The major difference is in the mix, the quantities of ingredients and the process of making the foodstuff fit to eat.

They can be stuffed into small sheep casings and large hog or beef ones, but they are not always linked. They are frequently tied with butchers twine so they can be hung or smoked or boiled.

Sausages that are smoked in order to preserve them also take up the flavour of the smoke and frequently this is the real reason for smoking them in the first place. You can buy smoke flavours to be added to your food, but this is not a preserving method, just an extra flavouring.

Smoking has always been an excellent way of preserving meat. The particles are toxic to bacteria, the wood oils which are unburned impregnate the food and act as a preservative. This kind of smoking is called cold smoke. The smoke is separated from the heat source and is brought to the food cool. The food is not cooked, it is smoked.

There are a number of smoking assemblies and a large number of plans available for home made smokers.

Essentially you need a clean container which is fed with smoke from a wood burning fire. Many old country cottages have smoking racks high in the chimney. The whole point is to present the smoke cold to the food. The process often takes around 24 hours.

The fuel that creates the smoke should be deciduous: oak chippings, hickory, apple, beech. Do not use highly resinous woods such as pine since it adds a flavour which is not appealing and the resin that remains unburned in the smoke will stick to the sausage, making it sticky and consequently very black.

You can buy various smoking blends in the form of different collections of wood chips from suppliers which are pre-mixed for particular foods. Experiment and you will find that smoking different kinds of sausages with the same wood will impart a flavour that is quite surprisingly unique.

You can add various mixes to the wood or alternatively honey to make a sweet smoke.

The other kind of smoking is called hot smoke. This cooks the food as well as imparting smokiness at around 80° Celsius. There are a number of hot smokers available on the market. The most popular ones are the cooker top variety which burn powdered wood. These machines are capable of hot smoking a kilo of sausage at a time. More commercial, barrel type hot smoking set ups will cope with more. But are consequently more expensive. Normally, hot smoked products are to be eaten very shortly after they have been prepared, but with the right amount of curing chemicals, they can be dried and stored.

Making Dried Sausages

Modern houses are ill equipped for drying sausages. The basics of preparing these sausages is to have a cool dry place that has no infestations of animals or fungi, and can remain dry for at least a month, preferably longer.

The fundamental rule is that you need a space that is at a temperature of 15° Celsius and 70% humidity. Some people use old fridges, some use their roof space. You are looking for a weight loss in your final sausage of around 30%.

The production of dried sausage depends on the addition of preservatives as well as taking water from the food. This two pronged approach is important, and the addition of saltpetre and ordinary salt is important if you are going to sell your sausages in certain markets.

It is not possible to use just any old salt; anti-caking agents such as Calcium carbonate, that allow the free flow of salt in a cruet, affect the cure. Use only curing salt.

In making dried sausages you cannot guarantee to actually kill all the bacteria every time, and so the young, those with weakened immune systems and the elderly might just be susceptible. If you are at all unsure it is recommended that you gain experience at cooking sausage for drying first and then progress to uncooked ones.

Of course, you cannot make fermented sausage in this way. These sausages are preserved by lactic acid in the mixture which is given off by beneficial microbes inside the mix. As a part of the mix you add a culture which begins to grow inside the sausage and the microbial acids leach into the sausage. These sausages are frequently also washed with penicillin culture to give them a white bloom on the skin. Of course, the culture growing inside adds a tangy flavour to the sausage.

It is a lot like brewing beer or fermenting wine. The build up of chemicals in the sausage inhibits the growth of the culture, and will eventually kill it altogether.

When the sausages are drying, hanging in whatever system you have, do not be surprised if they become mouldy. Here the nose is a really important tool. Unless they smell horrid, rancid or basically like off meat, then they are most probably fine to eat. It takes about a month, perhaps a little longer, to dry sausages sufficiently to make them edible. Avoid handling them, but check them every few days.

During this time the curing chemicals in a standard recipe kill the bacteria by osmotic pressure. This is increased as the water escapes from the sausage as it dries. Recipes also call for various other preserving ingredients from alcohol to strong spices. As the sausage dries the flavours not only intensify, but the meat settles and the texture improves.

Nitrite in Meat

In an earlier chapter we talked about leaving out saltpetre, but in dried sausages this is largely impossible. In the USA dried sausages that are sold have to, by law, contain a certain quantity of saltpetre.

Common salt preserves meat by osmotic pressure and the effect on the chloride on the cell walls of bacterial and fungal spores. Sodium nitrite, saltpetre, reacts in the meat to produce Nitric oxide, and this chemical attaches to protein in the meat to give it a bright red colour.

You are aiming at a level of no more than 200 parts per million nitrite, that is a five thousandth of the other products in the sausage, so if you are making 10 kilos of sausage you will need to carefully mix 2g nitrite thoroughly through the whole batch of sausage. For this reason we strongly recommend that you use ready mixed cures.

There are many commercial cures available for making dried sausages which contain exactly the right proportions of chemicals so you do not have to worry about the effectiveness of the cure. It goes without saying that cures should be stored in airtight containers, and well away from children.

The Drying

This needs to take place in a cool room. You can buy (or make) dryers of various kinds, but they must be cool dryers. This is a slow process; you do not want to force the water from the sausage in a matter of just a few hours. (That said, you can buy dehumidifiers which do the job quickly for certain sausages).

Sausages that are hung to dry should not be touching each other and the free flow of cool air should be maintained.

The traditional time for drying sausages was after the pig

slaughter in Autumn, so there was much more likelihood of getting the right temperature for drying. Summer time hanging is much more likely to spoil, particularly in the UK climate of reasonably high temperature and an awful lot of rainfall.

How do you know it's done?

There is no real answer to that and to a degree it depends on the thickness of the casing and the thickness of the sausage. Most recipes state leaving them for a month or six weeks, when they will 'look' right and the flavours will have had time to mature as well as killing any resident bacteria.

7 Chapter Seven
Sausage Types

There are hundreds of traditional varieties of sausage, and even more speciality ones. Of course the number of sausages that can be made is limited only by the imagination.

In the UK the sausage has long been a part of everyone's diet, and there is a bewildering array of gourmet delicacies from the UK. Above all the British sausage is succulent, full of juice and flavour. It is about time that we celebrated British food and locally produced raw materials. It is a well known fact that our beef is the best in the world; that our pork and chicken is farmed in the most humane way possible and that our seafood, possibly the real reason why the Romans invaded these lands, is incomparable. Quite literally, no one has food like ours anywhere on the planet. Yet we allow the French, the

Spanish, the Italians, the Americans and almost anyone else to hoodwink us into believing traditional British food is somehow inferior to theirs.

It is impossible to compare a chorizo to a breakfast sausage and say which is better. Sausage varieties are so different in nature, but where else would you find over 200 recipes for what you might call breakfast sausage than the UK? Many of the recipes have been developed over centuries and are dependant on particular meat from a very close locality seasoned with the spices that grow most abundantly in that area.

One common thread for British sausages is the flavour of sage, particularly the Lincolnshire sausage that is crammed with the stuff! Lincoln sausages are traditionally thick linked, that is made into large sausages. More modern types have been served much thinner.

Sage grows well in most parts of the UK. But less well in cooler, wetter Scotland, though it is still used north of the border.

Various meats are traditional, of course, and pork is the favourite, but the Oxford sausage, for example, has veal while others have chicken, beef or lamb.

Somerset sausages are made using cider – sometimes with chunks of apple in the mixture, which makes them very special, and the pork is traditionally from the Saddleback pig.

Hogg's pudding is a West Country haggis type of sausage with barley as a basic constituent, made with all kinds of cuts of meat including caul, pluck (finely minced heart and lungs), kidney, face and trotter. It is stuffed into large hog casings and sewn. (Our version is somewhat simpler and has a touch of garlic)

Cumberland sausage has never been linked, and as such is a throw back to medieval times. It is simply wound into a long coil and sometimes staked with a skewer. It is spiced with pepper and cooked in a coil in the pan.

Northumbrian sausages are flavoured with leek. Leek has long been a favourite vegetable in the Northeast, where it is grown in competitions for large amounts of cash.

Gloucestershire sausage is made from Gloucester Old Spot pork with mace, sage, thyme, marjoram and black pepper. Some recipes call for mustard powder. Another Gloucester sausage, Stow sausage, is a mixture of pork and game – usually venison. They also make Stow pies.

Glamorgan sausages have Caerphilly cheese in them – there are recipes for vegetarian ones. The use of cheese as a fat substitute is quite common as it gives a creamier sausage. If you are making this kind of sausage, try to use half-fat or Dutch cheese. Cheddar, for example, is so full of fat that the sausage would be too oily.

Cambridge sausages are flavoured with a small amount of nutmeg and ginger and were first eaten at the University.

The Marylebone sausage is a traditional London sausage that has a number of different spices depending on the district, usually mace, ginger and sage.

Lorne sausage, or square sausage, sometimes referred to as a slice, is a square sausage that was invented by a Scottish comedian in the late Victorian period. It is made from a mixture of pork and beef and has a very smooth consistency. Scottish sausages traditionally are more finely ground than English ones and are frequently combinations of meat; pork and beef or pork and rabbit.

We have already mentioned in passing the sausage known as black pudding, which was first made in ancient times and is still enjoyed in surprising numbers. These are stuffed into large skins or even stomachs, as is haggis, a sausage made from offal and barley. Black pudding is a Lancashire dish, still eaten in large quantities in Bury, the centre of black pudding making. Examples of this delicacy are sent all around the world.

William Cobbett, the nineteenth centaury writer on self-sufficiency, said that a happy nation was created by having a 'pig in every home.' This was realised more in some counties than others. The geographical history of the sausage reflects this. Those counties where the local brand of sausage is not recognised tend to be the industrialised ones where the peasant communities were moved from the land and into the factories more efficiently.

An interesting feature of the British sausage is the response to the climate, and hence the agriculture of the region. For example, English sausages generally have wheat products, breadcrumbs and so on, as a binding agent. Welsh sausages tend to be restricted to the borders, Glamorganshire, Salop and so on, partly because there are precious few places to grow wheat in great quantities in the mountainous central regions of Wales, and partly because the predominant meat of Wales is lamb.

The further north you go the harder it is to grow good quality wheat, and consequently, Scottish sausage tends to be stuffed with barley or oats, save where the huge quantities of wheat brought in to the country from the 'old alliance' with France made breadcrumbs and wheat grain available around Edinburgh.

Sausages from Europe

This is not an exhaustive list, but it does give a basic idea of the major types of those available. There are many air dried Southern European types. Northern European ones tend to be smoked or cooked or steeped in brine.

Andouillette is a traditional French sausage made with a blend of pork and spices, including garlic. It is heavily smoked and uses the intestine of the pig as a major constituent. Andouille is considered an insult in France and some commentators suggest that it is related to the British term, 'silly sausage'. This sausage is around 50% stomach and intestine, spiced and smoked. It is cooked and sliced thinly.

Similarly, Toulouse a less highly spiced sausage of the type enjoyed in the south of the country, is usually put into stews and casseroles; only this one is more pork than stomach. It is often eaten in the popular French dish cassoulet.

Biroldo is a kind of black pudding from Northern Italy which is found in two forms; sweet and savoury. The

Most stuffing machines come apart for cleaning
and storage and need to be reassembled
each session.

The stuffer needs
to be securely at-
tached to the table
top before use
with a G Clamp.

Three different sizes of tube allow the making of sausages of many thicknesses.

When you attach the nozzle to the body, make sure the surfaces are clean and that it sits home securely, otherwise the sausage meat will pour out everywhere.

The casings are attached to a ring, or a string. Lift it up and the skins will collapse around each other and separate quite easily.

The casings can be washed inside by pouring water from the tap and allowing the 'bubble' to swill through the inside.

The end of the skin needs to be located—push your finger through it and then transfer to the nozzle.

Pull the open case over the nozzle and then draw the rest of the casing on.

Your sausage mixture is now ready for its final fate.

Exude the meat until it takes the skin. This sausage maker has tied the end of the casing, this is not always necessary.

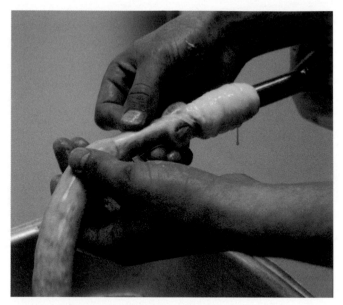

Do not allow the casings to over fill.

If you can, collect the sausage on a tray—the freer the sausage can be made the better.

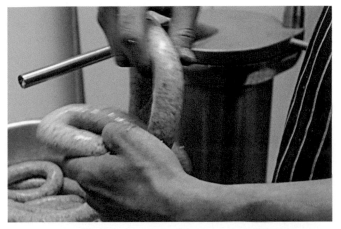

With practice you will be able to link at a
remarkable rate.

Link each length of casing before you start to fill
another.

Unused skins can
be salted, covered
and used again.

Well worth it!
(Cheshire sausage by Designasausage,
See resources pages for details).

former is pig's blood and raisins, the latter calf's blood with cheese.

Botifarra is a Spanish sausage, made from pork and air dried with cinnamon.

Boudin blanc is a pork and chicken sausage which is often cooked in milk and stuffed into large casings. It is very finely ground and spiced with a little pepper.

Bierwurst is not made from beer, but pork and beef and comes from many German areas and Austria. It is flavoured with brandy or rum.

Bresaola is a thinly sliced beef sausage, dried, spiced and stuffed into large ox casing.

Cervellata was traditionally a way of making pig brain more appetising. Its name means brain sausage, though it is not always made from this ingredient these days.

Cervelat is a German sausage made of pork and beef and lightly smoked.

Chorizo has become very popular in the UK. It is a Spanish sausage that has many varieties and is made from paprika, garlic and chillies.

Coppa is an Italian sausage popular in the UK and is flavoured with nutmeg.

Extremenza is a Spanish blood sausage bulked out with potato or squashes.

Frankfurters are fine textured, lightly smoked and then boiled. Of course, they come from Frankfurt in Germany. Knackwurst, Bockwurst and Bratwurst are all variations on the Frankfurter.

Katenrauchwurst is a coarse German sausage made from a variety of ingredients including offal. It is translated roughly as 'smoked cottage sausage.'

Loukanika is a Greek sausage probably of Roman origin. The Lucanians produced a sausage that travelled the Ancient world with the Roman Legions. It resembles a Cumberland sausage, but is spiced with chilli.

Mocetta is an Italian goat sausage with juniper berries and garlic. It is eaten thinly sliced.

Mortadello is a medieval sausage of Italy and France and has a complex recipe of pork, fat, olives, garlic and nuts of various kinds, all stuffed into a large Ox casing and then steamed.

Strasbourg sausage is a light coloured sausage made from pork and a wide range of spices and peppers. It is mixed with milk. It has a fine consistency, but with bits of meat in the mix.

Salami is a wide ranging sausage of many different types and varieties and is salt cured. Sometimes they are stuffed into Ox casings, other times Pig's bladders.

Sulzwurst is a brawn sausage which is spiced with garlic and comes from Germany. It is made, like all brawn, from pig face.

Thessalias are pork sausages from Greece that resemble Northumbrian sausages in that they are flavoured with Leek.

"HOT DOG"

The Origins of the Hot Dog

It seems strange that the word dog should be associated with sausages. However, in the late 1600s a German, Johann Georghehner, invented a little sausage that he called a Dachshund, or little dog. This became popular in Frankfurt and Vienna. An alternative name for the dog in the US is the Wiener, which is simply Austrian for a resident of that city.

As Germans moved to New York in the US, they took dachshund sausages with them, and these were sold on the streets from around 1875 onwards. A cartoonist, T .A. "Tad" Dorgan drew a picture of a vendor selling sausages in a bun that were shaped like dachshunds at a sporting event but because, it is said, he could not spell the word dachshund he simply wrote "hot dog!"

From this time on, like the Lucanian sausage of the Roman Empire, hot dogs have travelled around the world on the back of American culture.

⑧ Chapter Eight
What Makes a Good Sausage?

British sausages are succulent. We do not have much of a tradition of smoked, dry sausages in this country. The reason for this is that the humidity is frequently above 100% for days on end and the sausage simply tends to rot under the heavy burden of all that moisture. Imagine a Manchester dry sausage!

So, British sausages are parcels of meat, fat and flavourings such as herbs, some salt and possibly pepper and/or sugar and a certain quantity of cereal to bind the sausage and mop up all that tasty fat. Doesn't sound all that healthy does it? Well home made sausages really are healthy, but first let us look at the sausages you buy from the supermarket. I would like to stress that you can buy excellent sausages from supermarkets. As with everything else, 'you pays your money and takes your choice.'

What Makes a Cheap Supermarket Sausage?

Meat
The definition of what constitutes meat is based on new regulations. What is referred to as meat can be 25% fat and 25% connective tissue. Although this can be called meat, if you were to put it on a plate you wouldn't want to eat it.

The 'meat' content of cheap pork sausages is 40%. The amount of pork in a pork sausage might only be a quarter lean meat and this is exactly what you get with cheap supermarket sausages. Of course, you can pay extra for better ones.

Under new regulations you cannot call mechanically recovered meat, MRM, pork or beef or whatever. However, a pork sausage can contain 20% MRM – which is basically forced off the bone under high pressure and not really recognisable as meat as such.

Rusk
To bulk and bind and only a bad thing when in huge quantities.

Water
The cheapest material of all, added for all sorts of reasons, some of them valid such as making the sausage flow through the machinery properly, others completely bogus; why sell sausages when you can sell water?

Substances are also added to stop the water evaporating from the sausage, and therefore maintaining its palatability after an extended period on the shelf.

E Numbers

E100 - E199 are colour enhancers and dyes. They could be something as harmless as E101, which is Vitamin B2 or as in the case of E127, erythosine, have implications in photo-sensitivity and possibly carcogeneticity.

E200 - E299 are preservatives, largely to extend the shelf life and could be as innocuous as E201, sodium sorbate, which is produced naturally or like E218, methyl para-hydroxybenzoate or methyl paraben which has been found to have oestrogen-like properties and has been found accumulated in breast cancer tumours.

E300 – E399 are antioxidants and acidity buffers. These could be something like E300, ascorbic acid or Vitamin C, or in the case of E319 tert-butylhydroquinone be implicated in stomach ulcers in lab tests, DNA damage and a possible carcinogen.

E-numbered chemicals between E400 and E599 tend not to have any health consequences. However, you might be interested to hear that food can contain industrial substances – sulphuric acid, for example, is an additive which maintains acidity and is sometimes used in small quantities.

E400 – E499 are stabilisers, emulsifiers and thickeners.
E500 – E599 are anti-caking agents and buffers.
E600 – E699 are flavour enhancers.

E624 is the ubiquitous monosodium glutamate which my local take-away still uses by the bucketful and is a substance which has many metabolic functions and effects. I can only say that for me it makes my heart race and I can't sleep when I have eaten it.

What we are not told about is the origin of the additive, which might have some bearing on your decision about buying the product. For example, 27 of the chemicals in the list of E numbers are classified as being possibly or likely to have been sourced from genetically modified crops.

Lycopene E106d comes from tomatoes. It happens to be an excellent chemical for the treatment and prevention of testicular cancer. It is used as a colourant and sometimes comes from GM tomatoes.

Getting it Right

When we allow businesses to create our food for us we run the risk of eating a product that they consider to be economically viable and not necessarily just plain wholesome food. But now you're in charge.

A word about Salt

On the whole the amount of salt in all food has fallen recently. But this is an average figure based on the fact that some low salt foods have been introduced and their presence in the market place lowers the overall figure. However, where salt is added, it has increased dramatically over the last dozen or so years.

Some sausages contain as much as 33% of the recommended daily intake (and that's just from two sausages), and when you add up all the other food eaten during the day we regularly consume more than 300% of the recommended amount.

There are examples of sausages having a gram of salt each! Our recipes, where they are categorised as medium salt, have very much less than this, and much less again for the low salt ones.

Moreover, the above figures are for adults. The same two sausages would give more than half the daily intake of salt for a child.

When you make your own sausages, you control the amount of salt in them. In my opinion, tasty meat and fresh ingredients do not need so much salt in order to make them palatable. You can, if you wish, make no salt sausages.

Fat

Fat is an important food, we need to take it in our diet.

Sausages come from a time when almost everyone did strenuous manual labour for several hours a day and needed a diet rich in energy. There is no getting round the fact that most sausages do have a high fat content, but, as Delia Smith said when she made her ridiculously unhealthy but wonderfully tasty chocolate cake, "you don't have to eat this every day!"

However, it is possible to cut down or change the amount and the type of fat in the sausage! Saturated fat, the kind of fat that comes in belly pork, is not only implicated in weight gain, but also in altering the metabolism so that blood cholesterol increases. Trans-fats, which are created when certain vegetable oils are hydrogenated to create solid fat and certain margarines, are said to make this process even worse.

It is possible to reduce cholesterol by replacing these fats with unsaturated fats – sunflower oil, olive oil and fatty acids from fish oils. Some of our recipes call for full fat, old fashioned sausages; others replace the fat with olive oil or other substances such as nut oil.

Use Excellent Ingredients!

One of the best reasons for home made sausages is economics. You will not be able to make sausages as cheaply as the cheapest supermarket ones. Home made sausages are not a way of saving money in a frugal living sort of way. However, you can make the very best sausages, which would cost more than best steak in the shops, for a fraction of the cost. So there is little to be gained in using the cheapest meats to make your sausages.

There are some meat outlets, easily mistaken for butchers, who sell pre-frozen meat which is then allowed to warm up in order to serve it as ready cut meat. We have one locally that sells cubed pork. Whereas this meat is perfectly safe and wholesome when cooked, as we have already discussed, the refreezing of meat has health implications. Be careful to freeze sausages only made from fresh meat.

If you are using your own animals that have been butchered, there is every reason to include in your grind the ear and face meat. They have been used for centuries in sausages, along with more luxurious cuts. The problem with 'ears and lips' arises when these ingredients represent the only or the most substantial part of the stuffing meat. From the point of view of the appropriate and respectful use of an animal killed for its meat and using the entire carcass, rather than throwing the head away it is much better to use the face meat in sausage; even if you have to pay the butcher to cut it up for you.

Pig

Good quality pork shoulder and well cut belly, leg and rib all make wonderful sausages. Pork loin is very lean and ideal for using in fat free or low fat sausages, although you might need more flavourings. Other cuts from the pig, as we have already discussed, are perfectly acceptable and include trotter, face, ears, snout, tongue and pluck (though this is rarely used these days). Liver and kidney are also used and, of course, intestine for casings.

It is not recommended that you try to use the intestine of a home butchered pig. Bought skins are subject to microbial testing, and are made in such a way as to ensure the safety of the operator.

Ham and bacon are also used in sausages. In these recipes, use only the very best dry cured bacon and ham.

Finally; a word about blood. You cannot buy blood fresh from the butchers. It's not allowed. You can collect the blood of your own pigs from the abattoir or you can obtain dried blood, which must be hydrated. There are special instructions for using this wonderful ingredient in the recipes for black pudding.

You might not want to use blood directly to make your

own black pudding, but you can use bought black puddings to make sausage. See our recipe for a mixture sausage of minced pork and black pudding in a simple 50/50 mixture.

Beef

Almost the same can be said for beef sausages in relation to cuts of meat. Shin is a frequent ingredient, as is rib and neck. If you really want to make sausages from the prime cuts, and why not – sirloin and brie – wow!, you might need the addition of a little fat. Oxtail sausages are fun, if a little messy to get the meat from the bone. Ox heart is a wonderful meat for sausages, particularly when mixed with other cuts to dilute the strong flavour. It adds a gamey savouriness to your ordinary cuts of meat.

Lamb

This is an oily meat with a strong flavour. It lends itself to fruity or mint sausages and the best cuts are neck, shoulder or leg. It is such a shame that Lamb carcasses are currently low in value to farmers and many currently use good cuts of meat to add value in sausages. Strangely, lamb often needs the addition of fat. Lamb fat melts so easily and can disappear in cooking. The sausage then shrinks and you are left with a shrivelled skin.

Game

Game is an excellent meat for speciality sausage, particularly when mixed with other meats or fruit. Pigeon, rabbit or hare can be used but be careful about the nature and freshness of the game, which may well have been hung for up to ten days. Venison is such a lean meat that you can make very healthy sausages, or alternatively make a more expansive product by adding fat. Venison and

Stilton is a dream combination.

Wild Boar is, as you would imagine, just like pork – so much so as to make no difference, save it is a little more gamey, but not that much. Squirrel and hedgehog might appear to be a little over the top, but have been used in the past, as have snipe and woodcock. The old English maxim, treat it like chicken, seems to work reasonably well, except that smaller, dark meat game birds are not so fatty, and get tough when over cooked.

Vegetarian Sausages

Now don't get all upset when you read this! I personally cannot think of any reason for pretending some other protein, such as soy, is meat when it is clearly not. Why not give a soya sausage its real name? The most basic reason for making a vegetable sausage is to create a dish that is substantial on the plate that can either be sliced like meat would be or eaten like a sausage.

But there are many other reasons besides. A vegetable sausage, say for example sage, onion, sweet corn, grated carrot and breadcrumbs with a drop of sesame for savouriness and olive oil for succulence and salt and pepper can be a simply mouth-watering sausage!

What better way can there be of feeding the vegetarian in the family and at the same time making the carnivores jealous?

Vegetables that go into sausages should be fresh and un-bruised and you need to remember that you are creating more a dish for immediate eating than a food that is meant for storage. Raw materials such as potato and cabbage change nature when frozen so they will need to be kept in the fridge. Vacuum packing can extend their life somewhat.

It is also quite possible these days, though a little more troublesome, to get vegetarian skins.

So What Makes a Good Sausage?

Sausages should cook well, taste good and be wholesome. The recipes in this book have been tried and tested but when you are concocting your own you need to bear in mind three things. They must cook well, they must be stuffed with plenty of fresh, excellent ingredients and they must be regarded not as everyday staples, so be extravagant!

Cooking well, for British sausages, means they have a little moisture to enable them to fry well in very little oil. This moisture can come from fat as well as stock or water.

Notice how hot a spring roll has to get in order to cook its contents, and to be able to achieve this temperature it has to be deep fried. Make sure there are no air spaces in your sausages; that your ingredients are thoroughly mixed and that chunks of meat or other ingredients are kept to a reasonable size. You are trying to avoid a product that has different cooking times within the same sausage.

Chapter Nine
Selling Sausages

Among the most exciting food movements in the UK are the country fair and farmers' market. It gives the opportunity for a small farmer or smallholder to sell products that give added value to what they grow on the farm. A pig farm does not need enormous amounts of land and the added care and benefits a small producer can give to their animals should be very marketable in their final products.

For example, two or three breeding sows, kept organically and free range can produce a couple of dozen pigs a year and the belly, neck and shoulders of these animals can provide upwards of £1500s worth of sausages at 2006 prices, even more if you cook and sell them for immediate consumption.

You will have to be sure of the Local Environmental Health rules and regulations, you will need to have some basic hygiene certification and maintain a relationship with your local food inspector.

There is now no escape from Local Area Health Regulations. Under new legislation that is Europe-wide, everyone who wants to sell food must register their premises with the local authority. You are legally obliged to make sure your product is safe to eat and reasonable value for money, as well as being fit for the purpose it is sold for. However, you must be able to prove a number of factors to the Food Inspector.

First you will have to have in place a documented food safety system. This is not just a document that you can copy off the internet; you must be able to show that each of the statements in it are verifiably accurate.

They will want to know how you keep contamination, foreign bodies, and microbes out of the food; how you will be able to recognise that the product is being kept safe and how the food remains safe in transport and at the point of sale.

The point of Local Environmental Health regulations is that they reflect the locality, and so what is expected in one area might be similar but different to another. The very best advice is to contact your local authority and ask to speak to a Food Inspector. They will send you a booklet giving guidelines relevant to your business and area.

Basic Rules and Regulations

What follows might not apply to you, in fact in many cases it probably does not, so to repeat the mantra, check with your local authority.

Registration

You are required to register your premises as a food unit. This should be around a month before you start producing to allow time for the local authority to visit you and make sure you have all the relevant information. If you are obliged to register, and much depends on the accuracy of the information you give them at first, you will also have to register any changes you make in the future.

If you inform the food inspector that you make sausages once a week for sale at the local farmers market you will probably find that you have an easier process to follow than if you make sausages every day for sale in a shop; as such you will be categorised differently.

Hygiene

The Food Standards Agency give guidelines about the requirements for food hygiene that you must adhere to with regard to general cleanliness, control of infection, storage and the manufacturing process.

Even if you use your own kitchen you must make sure that surfaces are cleanable, equipment is properly stored and cleaned, pets and children have no access to cooking areas and the product is as infection free as can possibly be expected. You might be asked to prepare your sausages in a specially dedicated room with separate equipment and professional surfaces.

You will also be asked to demonstrate how effectively you would deal with unforeseen problems and manage food safety. Good practice does not simply just happen. You might be asked how you identify what might possibly go wrong, and what you could do about it. How do you check things are running well and how do you actually know your hygiene regime is working.

You may need to keep documents about cleanliness routines, particularly if there is more than one person actually making the sausages.

As well as the FSA and Local Environmental Health Inspector, your local butcher should be a source of invaluable information.

The resources section at the back of this book has details of where to get the most up to date food hygiene information.

Labelling

You are required to show exactly what is in your sausage. Here you are at an advantage over the commercial producer because they might not want to advertise the monosodium glutamate in their product. Your sausages will, as likely as not, contain all natural ingredients, and so it becomes a selling point.

If you use pre-mixed sausage spices, you will need to transfer the original manufacturer's information to your label. However, many pre-mixed spices are very natural in their content, so there is no need to panic too much.

Presentation and Packing

You really cannot afford to skimp here. Buy some professional trays and good quality display cabinets. This should be built into your business plan – people do not buy sausages from a pasting table made by someone in a shell suit. Buy professionally painted 'A' frame advertising boards and even make a stand which matches the image you are trying to give.

Learn to tie sausages in threes for the basic, bread and butter, sausage – which of course should be a lot better than you can buy in the supermarkets. Luxury sausages can be displayed singly.

Vacuum packaging can work for dried sausages, but for traditional wet sausages can look a little odd – liquid leaches out of the sausage and into the plastic. This puts people off so they are best kept in the traditional manner.

Hand cut sausages, wrapped in butchers plastic or serving paper, folded into a neat parcel is by far the best way of presenting gourmet sausages.

Information is the keyword. Give as much as you can about your product, because this is how it sells. When people buy in packets from the supermarket they glance at the name of the product, look at the colour and then compare the price.

At the farmers market people look at the product and congratulate themselves on buying a product which is traditional, good for them, helping the farmer or is simply delicious. Generally, the price comes a little further down on the shopper's list.

10 Chapter Ten
Sausage Recipes

These notes contain some important hints and tips and are a valuable read before making a start with the recipes.

All these recipes are per kilo of meat, which will make around 8 – 12 hog cased sausages and around double to three times this amount if stuffed into sheep's intestines. It is convenient when just starting out to buy a single kilo of meat and bash away. You will soon wish to make larger batches, and so each recipe page has the quantities for 5 kilos. These quantities are easily multiplied up when making more than the quantity in the recipe.

It is not always practical to make a kilo of dried sausage, and so you will find, from time to time, the quantities change in individual recipes.

High	
Med	Fat, Salt
Low	Fat

The chart at the top of each page gives at-a-glance information about the basic nature of the sausage and it could be an idea to adapt this for your labels if you are going to sell your sausages.

Measurements

All these measurements are approximate to within a few grams for ease of measure. If you are converting some American recipes that are freely available on the internet or in the numerous books on sausage making that come from across the Atlantic, then you will need to convert cups of dry weight – 1 cup of breadcrumbs weighs around 125g, and 1 cup of rusk weighs around 150g, or thereabouts.

You can be further sure that you are adding the right amount of breadcrumbs or rusk if you remember that they constitute around 15% of the total weight of the ingredients. If you happen to add too much cereal by 50g on a 1 kilo mixture, you will not even notice it. But if you add too little the consistency might suffer.

You can use the weights of salt and pepper to 'guesstimate' the weight of most other condiments or spices by using your kitchen sense.

US measures are slightly larger than UK or Imperial measures, but not so much that it really makes a lot of difference, and the recipes and the conversions below have taken this into account.

Imperial or US	Metric
1 lb	0.45 Kg (450 g)
1 oz	28 g
1 pint	0.47 l or 470 ml
1 cup (2 cups per pint)	240 ml
1 tablespoon	15 ml
1 teaspoon	5 ml
1 teaspoon of salt	5 g
1 teaspoon of pepper	2.5 g
1 dash	0.5 g

Using Bought Sausage Spice

I might get chased, like the cartoon dog who has just stolen a string of sausages, by butchers all over the country when I tell you that, on the whole, the sausages you buy as 'award winning' sausages in many butchers' shops are no more than meat, rusk, water and pre-mixed spices from a factory somewhere.

Well probably there are one or two that are not like that, who make their sausages from raw ingredients but in preparation for this book I spoke to around a hundred sausage producers and very few did not use bought in spice mixes.

There is nothing wrong with making your own sausages in this way, indeed there are many manufacturers out there producing excellent mixes for all kinds of sausage. All you do is supply and grind the meat and perhaps some fat, rusk and water.

The recipes are generally as easy to follow as the basic sausage mix and simply call for weighing out the appropriate amount of herbs and spices. They should be stored in air tight containers and kept away from children.

A number of these mixes are indeed 'award winning' and make excellent sausages. They usually contain just the right amount of salt and any other curing compounds that might be necessary.

If you are going to make home cured dried sausage you will do no better than to buy in the spice mix and then you can be assured of a professionally blended product.

Your first forays into the world of sausage making will be very successful with a spice mix, many of which are totally organic. It is also possible to buy specialist mixes, vegetarian, gluten and allergy free.

Some of the recipes state that the meat should be ground coarsely, others fine. This is translated as being roughly chopped in a food blender to very finely chopped to a paste. The various plates on a grinder are marked coarse, medium or fine. The holes simply get smaller. You may well find that you need to grind your ingredients coarsely before they will go through the grinder with the fine disc in place.

As always, cooking is about taste. These recipes are there as a guide and you might think them bland or rich according to your taste. Do not think that the recipes are fixed; get a pencil out and scribble over them with your own amendments and variations.

If you are at all worried about being able to mix the ingredients, especially where there are tiny quantities, such as half a gram, then whisk them into water, either that called for in the recipe, or a small extra amount. This will reasonably ensure an even measurement.

The recipes in this book do not include information about cooling or freezing the meat before grinding. This simply to encourage readers to just get on with making sausages without the complexities of putting the meat into the fridge, removing it, returning it to the fridge etc.

Needless to say, meat grinds best when it is chilled, and you can take this into consideration when following the recipes, either by cubing the meat ready for grinding the night before or by some other method.

Fat is particularly difficult to grind because it can start to melt in the process. When you grind fat and meat together, the fat can melt and smear into the meat. This is best avoided by chilling the fat.

Andouille Sausage

High	Garlic, Pepper
Med	Salt
Low	

This is a French hot smoked sausage that some people say actually originated in Germany. There are a number of recipes which avoid the smoking, and the sausage is sliced and fried before serving. There is a lot of garlic in this sausage.

INGREDIENTS	METHOD
Basic Filling 1kg Pork shoulder 10 Chopped garlic cloves 200g Pork fat 200g tripe	Roughly grind the pork and fat. Grind the tripe finely. Thoroughly mix the meat with the dry ingredients.
Seasoning 20g Salt 20 Cracked black peppercorns 20g Cayenne pepper	Stuff into casings, knotting the ends of each link, approximately 30cm per sausage. Hot smoke for 3 to 4 hours.
Casings 2 metres of beef casing, soaked for at least 2 hours and washed inside and out.	You can add liquid smoke to the mix and refrigerate the sausage ready to fry slices as required.

Tip: Try adding a couple of tablespoons of honey to the mix.

Baking Chorizo

High		
Med	Chilli, Garlic Salt	
Low		

There are hundreds of recipes for this sausage. This one is not dried but kept frozen and cooked before use. It is moderately heavy on the chilli and garlic, so have a glass of something soothing nearby.

INGREDIENTS

Basic Filling
1kg Pork shoulder
50ml Cider or white wine

Seasoning
25g Salt
25g Mild chilli powder
6 Crushed and diced garlic cloves
10g Crushed cumin seed
5g Crushed oregano

Casings

2 metres of sheep casing, soaked and washed inside and out.

METHOD

Cube and grind the pork very finely

Combine all the other ingredients and knead the mix to ensure even mixing.

Fill into sheep skins and link as required. Traditionally they are long linked.

Freeze the sausages to store and bake them in the oven before use at 175° Celsius for 20 minutes, Gas mark 4.

They can be eaten hot or cold.

Tip: Wear plastic gloves when kneading.

Basic Breakfast Sausage

High	
Med	
Low	Fat, Salt, Seasonings

This basic sausage can be adapted to various recipes. It has a high meat to fat and salt ratio, and you can alter these according to your requirements. You can freely vary the cut of pork, or even go half pork and half of any other meat.

INGREDIENTS	METHOD
Basic Filling 1kg Pork shoulder 200g Pork Fat 100g Breadcrumbs or rusk 150ml Water	Thoroughly mix the dry ingredients so that the salt and pepper are completely incorporated. Finely mince the meat and fat.
Seasoning 5g Salt 5g Black pepper	Mix with the dry ingredients and the water.
Casings 2 metres of sheep casing, soaked and washed inside and out.	Stuff into casings and link as required. Leave for 24 hours to mature.

Tip: Try with 50g finely chopped sage or half a bunch of very finely chopped spring onions or five chopped garlic cloves.

Bierwurst Sausage

High	
Med	Salt
Low	Fat

This is a traditional sausage from Germany, but is repeated all over the continent. It is hot smoked until the centre of the sausage reaches a temperature of 75° Celsius for at least 30 minutes. It can then be frozen or refrigerated before use. It will keep for a couple of weeks but be careful not to leave it too long.

INGREDIENTS

Basic Filling
1kg Pork shoulder
1kg Shin beef
500g Belly pork
100ml Brandy

Seasoning
35g Salt
20g Sugar
6 Crushed garlic cloves
5g White pepper

Casings
3 metres of large hog casing, soaked for at least an hour and washed inside and out.

METHOD

Very finely grind all the meat, making sure there is nothing stringy left in the process.

Combine all the ingredients in a large bowl until everything is thoroughly and evenly mixed.

Stuff into casings, being careful to avoid air pockets and tie each sausage.

Hot smoke for around an hour. Check with a sausage thermometer that the temperature has risen to 75° Celsius and has remained at this for at least thirty minutes.

Tip: Some recipes call for juniper berries and rum. Try mustard as a seasoning.

Black Pudding

	High	Fat, Salt
	Med	
	Low	

You can buy dried blood to make your own black puddings. It may look like a complex process, but is actually fairly straight forward once you are organised.

INGREDIENTS

Basic Filling
1.5 Litres Pigs blood
500g Oatmeal
500g Barley
500g Pork fat
225g Breadcrumbs or rusk
3 Finely diced onions

Seasoning
20g Salt
10g Black pepper
10g Coriander
10g Dried sage
10g Mace

Casings

2 metres of beef casing, soaked for at least two hours and washed inside and out.

METHOD

Soak the oatmeal overnight and boil the barley in a little salted water for 30 minutes.

Dice the pork fat into small pieces. Finely chop the onions and sweat in a little of the diced pork fat in a deep pan.

Add the oatmeal and the rest of the pork fat and cook for 15 minutes with the rest of the ingredients. Stir thoroughly and frequently.

Fill the casings (I use a spoon) and knot between links.

Plunge the sausages into gently boiling water. The puddings rise when nearly cooked, and they are finished when the liquid oozes brown.

Tip: The skins frequently split. Do not over stuff them and try to avoid air pockets.

Black Pudding Sausages

High	
Med	Fat, Salt
Low	

Making real black pudding might be a little gruesome for your liking, so try these made from bought black pudding and trimmed belly pork.

INGREDIENTS

Basic Filling

1kg Belly pork
1kg Black pudding
150ml Water

Seasoning

5g Salt
5g White Pepper

Casings

3 metres of hog casing, soaked for at least an hour and washed inside and out.

METHOD

Trim the skin off the belly pork and cube before grinding very finely.

Open the black pudding and scoop out the contents into a bowl and carefully mix with the other ingredients.

Fill into hog skins and link as required.

Tip: Use a mild black pudding to begin with. You can add mustard powder if you wish.

Boiled Beef Sausage

High	
Med	Salt
Low	Fat

These sausages are boiled before storage. They are fantastic with mustard. You can use a cut like shin, or any good lean beef. However, it is just as effective if you buy good lean minced beef.

INGREDIENTS	METHOD
Basic Filling 1kg Lean beef 150g Breadcrumbs or rusk 200ml Water 1 Egg **Seasoning** 7g Salt 5g Black pepper 5g Cayenne pepper 5g Dried sage **Casings** 2 metres of hog casing, soaked for at least an hour and washed inside and out.	Thoroughly mix the dry ingredients so that the salt, pepper and herbs are completely incorporated. Finely mince the meat or kneed ready minced beef. Mix with the dry ingredients and the water and beat in the egg. Stuff into casings and link as required. Cover with water in a pan and boil for 20 minutes. Dry and allow to cool before refrigerating.

Tip: These sausages are fried before serving. You can hot smoke them, or cook them in casseroles in a moderate oven.

Cambridge Sausage

High	Fat
Med	Salt
Low	

This sausage is nearly all meat, preferably Saddleback belly, which is quite fatty. Some recipes call for rice as the cereal, but we will stick to breadcrumbs or rusk.

INGREDIENTS

Basic Filling

1kg Belly pork (Saddleback if available)
75g Breadcrumbs or rusk
150ml Water

Seasoning

10g Salt
5g Black pepper
5g Nutmeg

Casings

1.5 metres of hog casing, soaked for at least an hour and washed inside and out.

METHOD

Thoroughly mix the dry ingredients so that the salt, pepper and nutmeg are completely incorporated.

Roughly mince the meat. You might wish to cut the skin off and finely grind it.

Mix with the dry ingredients and the water.

Stuff into casings and link as required.

Tip: Some recipes call for ginger. Use 5g of dried or 10g of fresh.

Chipolata Sausages

High	
Med	Fat
Low	Salt

This tiny sausage dates from the very early Regency period. From it the British banger was developed. They are ideal for parties and look much better than those boxes of machine made ones.

INGREDIENTS

Basic Filling

1kg Pork shoulder
150g Pork fat
200g Breadcrumbs or rusk
200ml Water

Seasoning
10g Salt
10g White pepper
5g Sage
5g Mace

Casings

2 metres of sheep casing, soaked and washed inside and out.

METHOD

Thoroughly mix the dry ingredients so that the salt, pepper and herbs are completely incorporated.

Finely grind the pork and fat and mix with the dry ingredients and the water.

Stuff into casings and link into small sausages, around an inch long with lots of twists.

Tip: You can either boil or bake them. They do not look good blackened in the frying pan.

Christmas Sausages

High	
Med	
Low	Fat, Salt

Try these as your Christmas sausages instead of chipolatas wrapped in bacon.

INGREDIENTS	METHOD
Basic Filling	Finely grind the pork and roughly grind the turkey and then combine the two.
500g Pork shoulder	
500g Turkey	
250g Breadcrumbs or rusk	Roughly chop the cranberries
150ml Water	
50ml Brandy	
	Combine all the other ingredients together.
Seasoning	
15g Salt	
10g Black pepper	
50g Cranberry	Stuff into casings and link as chipolatas.
20g Sugar	
	You can bake these in the oven from raw with your turkey roast.
Casings	
2 metres of sheep casing, soaked and washed inside and out.	

Tip: Merry Christmas!

Cumberland Sausage

High	
Med	Pepper, Salt
Low	

This traditional peppery sausage is quite highly seasoned. It dates back to before the time of the Reformation. You can vary it with roughly chopped sage and parsley.

INGREDIENTS	METHOD
Basic Filling 500g Belly pork 500g Pork shoulder 100g Breadcrumbs or rusk 100ml Water	Thoroughly mix the dry ingredients so that the salt, pepper and herbs are completely incorporated. Roughly grind all the pork.
Seasoning 10g Salt 10g Black pepper 5g Nutmeg A dash of dried sage A dash of mace	Mix with the dry ingredients and the water. Stuff into casings but do not link. You might need a second pair of hands to help you coil the sausage on to the tray.
Casings 2 metres of hog casing, soaked for at least an hour and washed inside and out.	

Tip: It is quite a tricky job to fry a full round Cumberland sausage. You might try baking in it a moderate oven.

Curried Beef Sausage

High	
Med	Spice
Low	

You can make perfect curried sausage by combining ground meat with a shop bought curry paste, or you can make your own spices using a lot of coriander.

INGREDIENTS

Basic Filling

1kg Shin beef
300g Breadcrumbs or rusk
150ml Water

Seasoning
10g Salt
25g Crushed coriander seed
10g Ground fenugreek seed
10g Cayenne pepper
10g Crushed cumin
5g Crushed black pepper

Casings

1.5m hog casing, soaked for at least an hour and washed inside and out.

METHOD

Grind all your seeds in a pestle and mortar and combine with the salt.

Finely grind the beef and thoroughly mix all the ingredients.

Stuff into casings and link as required.

Leave for a few hours for the flavours to blend.

These are great baked in a slow oven.

Tip: Serve with mango chutney, what else?

Duck and Pork Sausage

High	
Med	Fat
Low	Salt

These dark sausages are easy to make. They are an offshoot of our favourite Sunday roast dinner. You could include some pieces of orange, or make an oriental version with oyster sauce.

INGREDIENTS

Basic Filling
1kg Duck breast
1kg Belly pork
200g Breadcrumbs or rusk
200ml Water

Seasoning

25g Salt
10g Black pepper
10g Sugar
10g Thyme

Casings

3 metres of hog casing, soaked for at least an hour and washed inside and out.

METHOD

Freeze all the cubed meat prior to very fine grinding.

Mix all the ingredients carefully in a large bowl.

Stuff into hog casings and link as required.

Some recipes call for cold smoking of the sausages but they're just as good fried in a pan. The extra fat provided by the belly pork stops the filling from shrinking within the sausage.

Tip: These sausages are fantastic baked like a pot roast around a turkey or a beef joint.

Fat Turkey Sausage

High	
Med	Fat
Low	Salt

Turkey is a dry meat, as everyone knows on Boxing Day. This recipe calls for the addition of pork fat and is very lightly spiced with salt and pepper. It is a starter for other flavours and is easily modified.

INGREDIENTS	METHOD
Basic Filling	Finely mince the turkey meat and coarsely mince the fat.
1kg Turkey breast 300g White breadcrumbs 500g Chopped pork fat 200ml Water	Combine all the other ingredients.
Seasoning	Stuff into hog casings and link as required.
15g Salt 10g White pepper	
Casings	
1.5 metres of hog casing, soaked for at least an hour and washed inside and out.	

Tip: You can add 5g each of paprika, chilli or other flavours such as leek, garlic or spring onion.

Frankfurter

High	
Med	Salt
Low	

This is the typical German sausage, mildly flavoured and fine textured. They became the hot dog, the bratwurst and all the other types. They are sometimes filled with offal and heart is particularly called for in many recipes.

INGREDIENTS

METHOD

Basic Filling

1kg Pork shoulder
200g Breadcrumbs or rusk
200ml Water

Seasoning
15g Salt
5g White pepper
5g Mustard powder
5g Powdered mace
5g Paprika

Casings

2 metres of sheep casings, soaked and washed inside and out.

Roughly grind the pork and thoroughly combine all the dry ingredients.

Mix the meat with the dry ingredients and the water and regrind to make a finely ground paste.

Stuff into casings and link at around twice the ordinary length.

You can boil these sausages and eat them hot or cold.

Tip: Some recipes call for garlic, some call for ginger and others for extra fat.

Garlic Pepper And Pork Sausage

High	
Med	Chilli, Garlic, Salt
Low	Fat

The food of Cuba is renowned for being hot! This sausage combines traditional chilli with Chinese sweet chilli sauce to create a hot sausage.

INGREDIENTS

Basic Filling

1kg Belly pork
200g Breadcrumbs or rusk
200ml Water

Seasoning

15g Salt
10g Crushed chilli peppers
5g Black pepper
20 ml Sweet chilli sauce
6 Crushed and ground garlic cloves

Casings

2 metres of sheep casing, soaked and washed inside and out.

METHOD

Cut the skin off the pork.

Roughly grind the meat and very finely grind the skin.

Combine all the dry ingredients to ensure an even mix and then thoroughly mix all the rest.

Stuff into sheep casing and link into long sausages.

Tip: These can be cooked in the oven or pan and eaten hot or cold. Well, actually they can only be eaten hot, even when cold!

Glamorgan Sausage

High	
Med	Fat
Low	Salt

This version is a vegetarian sausage that is not stuffed, but rolled in breadcrumbs and bound with an egg. It makes a great sausage fest when served with other sausages.

INGREDIENTS	METHOD

Basic Filling

450g Caerphilly cheese
300g White breadcrumbs
2 Eggs

Seasoning

50g Finely chopped leek
15g Finely chopped chives

Casings

None required

Thoroughly mix all the ingredients, but only one of the eggs.

Beat the other egg in a bowl.

Roll sausage sized portions and dip in egg and then roll in some spare breadcrumbs.

These sausages can be fried for 10 minutes until the breadcrumbs and the egg are cooked.

You can use almost any crumbly white cheese but avoid Cheddar or other oily ones which will separate during cooking.

Tip: Some recipes call for Spring onion instead of Leek.

Gloucester Sausage

High		
Med	Fat, Pepper, Salt	
Low		

This can easily be called Farmhouse sausage. The use of suet as a fat is not restricted to Gloucestershire.

INGREDIENTS

Basic Filling

1kg Pork shoulder
225g Breadcrumbs or rusk
350g Suet
250ml Water

Seasoning

15g Salt
10g Black pepper
10g Finely chopped sage
A dash of nutmeg
A dash of marjoram

Casings

2 metres of hog casing, soaked for at least an hour and washed inside and out.

METHOD

Mix the dry ingredients thoroughly so that the salt, pepper and herbs are completely incorporated.

Finely grind all the pork and the suet.

Mix with the dry ingredients and the water.

Stuff into casings as required.

Tip: When you cook these sausages you do not need oil, the suet clarifies easily and lubricates the pan nicely.

Haggis

High	
Med	Fat, Salt
Low	

This is the traditional offal dish of Scotland. A sheep's pluck is the heart and lungs and sometimes includes the liver. You can add any number of spices to this basic recipe. In Scotland, they're probably a secret.

INGREDIENTS

Basic Filling

1 Sheep's pluck
500g Oatmeal
250g Finely chopped suet
4 Finely diced large onions

Seasoning

20g Salt
15g Black pepper
20g Mixed herbs
20g Allspice

Casings

Sheep's stomach, washed and soaked in salted water for 8 hours. Butchers twine for sewing the stuffed stomach.

METHOD

Boil the pluck in a large pan for 2 hours. Save 200ml of the liquid. Once cool, cut into small pieces and grind finely.

Mix all the dry ingredients until they are evenly distributed.

Combine the pluck and suet with the dry ingredients and the stock.

Mix well to make sure the pluck meat is not all heart in one place and lung in another.

Stuff into the stomach making sure there is room for the contents to expand. It helps also if it is pricked.

Simmer in boiling water for

Tip: You might want to cut out the windpipe.

Hogs Pudding

High	
Med	Spices
Low	Fat, Salt

This is a traditional Cornish sausage which has as many recipes as there are villages in the region. Some, like this one, ideally call for Ransoms, the wild form of garlic, grown in abundance in Cornwall and you can use the whole plant instead of just the corm.

INGREDIENTS

Basic Filling
1kg Pork shoulder
200g Boiled barley
200ml Water

Seasoning
5g Salt
5g Black pepper
5g Cumin
5g Oregano or basil
2 Finely chopped garlic cloves or ransoms if available.

Casings
2 metres of hog casing soaked for at least an hour and washed inside and out.

METHOD

Thoroughly mix the dry ingredients so that the salt, pepper and spices are completely incorporated.

Finely mince the meat.

Mix with the dry ingredients and the water.

Stuff into casings and link as required.

You can add 5g of celery powder and onion powder, if you wish.

Link the sausages with knots and boil until cooked.

Tip: You can either re-cook these sausages, or eat them soon after

Irish Velvet Sausage

High		
Med	Spices	
Low		

This should be called the Dubliner. A good glass of Guinness, best beef and shallots should be enough to keep any macho man happy. You should serve this with mashed potato and thick onion gravy. I have added some olive oil to this recipe to help cook the shallots.

INGREDIENTS

Basic Filling

1kg Shin beef
300g Breadcrumbs or rusk
200ml Guinness
25ml Olive oil

Seasoning
20g Salt
10g Crushed black pepper
50g Finely chopped shallots

Casings

2 meters of hog casing, soaked for at least an hour and washed inside and out.

METHOD

Give the beer a good length of time to flatten. You don't want all those bubbles.

Finely grind the beef and thoroughly mix all the ingredients.

Stuff into casings and link as required.

Leave for a few hours for the flavours to blend.

Tip: Also great with mustard, or horseradish sauce.

Lamb and Mint Sausage

High	
Med	Salt
Low	

All kinds of flavours can be added to this classic sausage. Use lean meat and add fat. Fatty lamb shrinks when the fat renders in the cooking, so although it might seem strange adding fat to lamb, it is important.

INGREDIENTS

Basic Filling

1kg Lamb steak
200g Breadcrumbs or rusk
200g Pork back fat
200ml Water

Seasoning
15g Salt
5g Black Pepper
25g Chopped and rubbed mint

Casings

2.5 metres of sheep casing, soaked and washed inside and out.

METHOD

Thoroughly mix the dry ingredients so that the salt and pepper are completely incorporated with the breadcrumbs or rusk and the finely chopped mint.

Roughly mince the lamb and coarsely mince the fat.

Mix all the ingredients together.

Stuff into casings and link as required.

Tip: You can experiment with rosemary or sage. Try a small amount at first.

Lemon and Fennel Sausage

High	
Med	Spices
Low	Salt

This is a best seller of one of Rick Stein's food heroes, Lords of Middleton. It is really worth getting to know your local butcher. They will be really helpful in providing ideas as well as meat or seasoning and skins. This zesty sausage is really appetizing.

INGREDIENTS

Basic Filling

1kg Pork shoulder
200g Breadcrumbs or rusk

Seasoning
5g Salt
15g Crushed fennel seed
200ml Water
The juice and pulp of 1 lemon
Finely chopped lemon zest

Casings

1.5 metres of hog casing, soaked for at least an hour and washed inside and out.

METHOD

Thoroughly mix the dry ingredients so that the salt and lemon zest are mixed with the breadcrumbs.

Chop the flesh of the lemon, not the pith, and add to the breadcrumbs along with the zest.

Finely grind the pork and mix with the dry ingredients adding the water and lemon juice.

Stuff into casings, and link as required.

Hang to mature for around 2 hours.

Tip: Don't forget to remove the pips and buy un-waxed lemon.

Lincolnshire Sausage

High		
Med	**Salt**	
Low		

I suppose the Lincolnshire sausage should have been a poacher's sausage, crammed with rabbit and game of all kinds, but this highly flavoured recipe is probably just enough. Stolen game would probably have to be eaten quickly anyway.

INGREDIENTS

Basic Filling

1kg Pork shoulder
150g Breadcrumbs or rusk
150ml Water

Seasoning

10g Salt
5g Black pepper
15g Chopped and rubbed sage

Casings

2 metres of sheep casing, soaked and washed inside and out.

METHOD

Thoroughly mix the dry ingredients so that the salt, pepper and sage are completely incorporated.

Finely mince the meat.

Mix with the dry ingredients and the water.

Stuff into casings and link as required.

Leave for 24 hours to mature.

Tip: Try larger hog skins for a thicker sausage, increasing the amount of cereal by 100g and another 100ml water.

Liver Sausage

High	
Med	Fat, Salt
Low	

This is the traditional liver sausage which is cooked in water in the oven. It can be smoked and kept in the fridge for many weeks. It is great with a salad or a sandwich.

INGREDIENTS

Basic Filling
500g Pig's liver
500g Chicken's liver
250g Beef liver
500g Fatty bacon
250g Belly pork

Seasoning
40g Salt (For 2kg meat)
20g Black pepper
10g Nutmeg
10g Crushed mustard seed
4 Crushed garlic cloves

Casings
1 metre of beef middles, soaked for at least 2 hours and washed inside and out.

METHOD

Cook all the livers in boiling water for 10 minutes.

Grind the bacon and belly pork and combine all the meat. Mix thoroughly with the rest of the ingredients.

Regrind all the mixture on a fine setting.

Fill into beef middles and divide into 30cm sausages, knotting the ends securely.

Boil in water for an hour and then chill in iced water.

Tip: Perfect with mustard.

Lucanian Sausage

High	
Med	Salt, Spice
Low	

This is the original Roman sausage, a recipe over two thousand years old. It calls, originally, for fish sauce and a roman condiment that is not readily available. Chinese fish sauce contains spices not available in the original.

INGREDIENTS

Basic Filling

1kg Belly pork
300g Breadcrumbs or rusk
150ml Water or stock
100g Crushed almonds

Seasoning
20g Salt
10g Crushed black pepper
20g Finely chopped parsley
10g Crushed cumin
10g Ground oregano

Casings

2 meters of hog casing, soaked for at least an hour and washed inside and out.

METHOD

Roughly grind the pork and crush the almonds in a pestle and mortar.

Thoroughly mix all the ingredients.

Stuff into casings and link as required.

Leave for a few hours for the flavours to blend.

Cook in a hot oven for 40 minutes or shallow fry.

Tip: Try with an ancient recipe of bean stew.

Malaysian Sausage

High	
Med	Fat
Low	Salt

This sausage was made by my friend Boon Hok when we were at University together. It contains five-spice powder. Come to think of it, everything he made had five-spice powder in it—even Christmas dinner once!

INGREDIENTS	METHOD
Basic Filling 1kg Pork shoulder 200g Pork fat 200g Breadcrumbs or rusk 150ml Water 10ml Fish sauce	Cube and grind the pork very finely. Very roughly chop the fat. Combine the five-spice powder with the breadcrumbs and the salt.
Seasoning 10g Salt 5g Five-spice	Combine all the other ingredients.
Casings 2 metres of sheep casing, soaked and washed inside and out.	Fill into sheep skins and link as required.

Tip: Try replacing some of the pork with an equal amount of Char Siu.

Manchester Sausages

High	
Med	Salt
Low	Fat

Along with Manchester Tart and Eccles cake, this is the only named foodstuff from the Athens of the modern world. It is a basic sausage with a little ginger powder. Alas, you will no longer find this in the shops.

INGREDIENTS

Basic Filling

1kg Pork shoulder
300g Breadcrumbs or rusk
200ml Water

Seasoning
20g Salt
5g White Pepper
1g Nutmeg
1g Mace
2g Ginger
2g Cloves

Casings

2 metres of hog casing, soaked for at least an hour and washed inside and out.

METHOD

Thoroughly mix the dry ingredients so that the salt, pepper and herbs are completely incorporated.

Finely grind the pork and mix with the dry ingredients and the water.

Stuff into casings and link as required.

Tip: Around 2 cloves make a gram, grind them in a mortar.

Marrow & Roast Vegetables

High	
Med	Salt
Low	

These sausages are so full of flavour and nourishment that they will keep you alive for ever. They are reasonably low salt, but do contain olive oil to help cook the contents.

INGREDIENTS	METHOD
Basic Filling 500g Marrow, peeled 200g Cubed carrot 200g Cubed parsnip 200g Whole roast garlic cloves 300g Breadcrumbs or rusk 200ml Vegetable stock 50ml Olive oil	Cube and par-boil the marrow until soft. Roast all the other vegetables until sweet in a medium oven. Grind or paste the marrows and mash the other veg with a fork.
Seasoning 20g Salt 10g White pepper	Thoroughly mix all the ingredients.
Casings 2m of hog casing, soaked for at least an hour and washed inside and out. Or you can use vegetarian skins.	Stuff into casings and link as required.

Tip: Use any sets of vegetables you have to hand.

Mediterranean style Sausage

High	
Med	
Low	Fat, Salt

This sausage is a real treat served hot or cold. You can make a really healthy sausage with lean beef and pork or just beef with a little extra oil.

INGREDIENTS	METHOD
Basic Filling 1kg Pork shoulder 200g Breadcrumbs or rusk 50g Chopped sun-dried tomatoes 150ml Water 10ml Olive oil	Cube and grind the pork very finely Roughly chop the tomatoes and combine all the other ingredients.
Seasoning 10g Salt 5g Chopped Basil 20g Tomato puree	Fill into sheep skins and link as required.
Casings 2 metres of sheep casing, soaked and washed inside and out.	

Tip: You can add a little honey for some extra sweetness.

Mushroom Sausage

High	
Med	Salt
Low	

This should really be called woodland sausage, or September sausage. Mushrooms make great vegetarian sausages, but you have to be careful not to grind them too much. Indeed, you don't really need a grinder.

INGREDIENTS

Basic Filling

1kg Assorted mushroom
300g White breadcrumbs
150ml Vegetable stock
50ml Extra virgin olive oil

Seasoning
20g Salt
10g Black pepper
The juice of 1 lemon

Casings
2 metres of thin vegetarian casing soaked and washed inside and out.

METHOD

Chop the mushrooms in to small pieces around 3mm.

Some mushrooms blacken on chopping, these you must chop more coarsely.

Sprinkle the cut mushrooms with lemon juice, salt and pepper.

Completely mix all the ingredients and stuff into casings .

Link as required.

Tip: Try shredding spinach into the mixture or onion or garlic. Also would be great with 50% mushroom/50% roast chestnut.

Northumberland Sausage

High	
Med	Salt
Low	

The North East of England is just as famous as Wales for growing leeks, where large amounts of prize money are still available for the best specimens. This sausage continues that tradition.

INGREDIENTS

Basic Filling

1kg Pork shoulder
200g Breadcrumbs or rusk
200ml Water
100g Finely chopped leek whites

Seasoning
10g Salt
5g Black pepper

Casings
2 metres of hog casing soaked for at least an hour and washed inside and out.

METHOD

Thoroughly mix the dry ingredients so that the salt and pepper are completely incorporated with the cereal.

Roughly mince the meat and mix well with the leek.

Mix with the dry ingredients and the water.

Stuff into casings and link as required.

Some recipes call for the leek to be sweated a little in fat before combining them, which makes them easier to cook in the final sausage.

Tip: You can add some sage to this recipe, or chives. Try to avoid using the green leaves of the leek; they can be tough.

Oxford Sausage

High	
Med	Fat
Low	Salt

There are many recipes for Oxfords. Some call for the cook to bind the mix with an egg and roll in flour to make sausage shapes. Others call for the roll to be in a caul of pig body fat. We are stuffing our version. You can replace the veal with chicken.

INGREDIENTS	METHOD
Basic Filling 500g Pork shoulder 500g Veal 300g Pork fat 225g Breadcrumbs or rusk 150ml Water	Thoroughly mix the dry ingredients so that the salt, pepper and herbs are completely incorporated.
Seasoning 10g Salt 5g Black pepper 5g Nutmeg 5g Dried sage	Finely grind the pork and veal. Finely chop the fat with a sharp knife. Mix with the dry ingredients and the water. Stuff into casings and link as required.
Casings 3 metres of sheep casing, soaked and washed inside and out.	

Tip: Try it with a hint of orange, and a little orange zest or lemon juice. You will be completely surprised.

Oyster Sauce Sausage

High	
Med	Salt
Low	Fat

This is a bit of a cheat. It uses no real oysters, save the ones put into the sauce. I love these sausages, especially because it doesn't really matter how much sauce you put in them. Although there is nothing in this but pork and sauce, it is quite high in salt.

INGREDIENTS	METHOD
Basic Filling	Just grind, combine and stuff!
1kg Pork shoulder	
200g Breadcrumbs or rusk	I think this is better with breadcrumbs than rusk.
150ml Oyster sauce	
	Link into fat sausages which are cooked in the oven and enjoy.
Seasoning	
	They do not keep very well.
Casings	
1.5 metres of hog casing, soaked for at least an hour and washed inside and out.	

Tip: Drizzle these sausages with honey, but I bet you can't eat three of them!

Pigeon Sausage

High	
Med	Salt
Low	

Those of you who shoot will know that, on a good day, you have too much pigeon. These are easy to cook sausages with a delicate flavour. They are good with ordinary sausages, adding just one for variation. They freeze well, but do not keep too long in the fridge.

INGREDIENTS	METHOD
Basic Filling 1kg Pigeon breast 500g Fat bacon 200g Breadcrumbs or rusk 200ml Water	Pigeon grinds best from frozen. Finely grind all the meat.
Seasoning 20g Salt 10g Black pepper 25g Chopped parsley	Completely mix all the ingredients and stuff into casings . Link as required.
Casings 2 metres of sheep casings, soaked and washed inside and out.	

Tip: This recipe can be used with any game. It is extremely simple. I prefer to make sausages from fresh meat, not hung.

Pork and Chive Sausages

High	
Med	Fat
Low	Salt

No garden is complete without a big stand of chives. They are fantastic for all kinds of dishes. These sausages are really flavoursome and succulent.

INGREDIENTS	METHOD
Basic Filling 1kg Pork shoulder 200g Pork fat 250g Breadcrumbs or rusk 200ml Water 50g Chopped chives	Finely grind the pork, roughly grind the cooled fat and then combine the two with all the other ingredients.
Seasoning 15g Salt 10g Black pepper	Stuff into casings and link as required.
Casings 2 metres of hog casing, soaked for at least an hour and washed inside and out.	

Tip: You can substitute belly pork for the fat if you prefer.

Pork and Onion Sausage

High	
Med	Fat
Low	Salt

This recipe needs really finely minced onion so that it cooks easily in the sausage.

INGREDIENTS	METHOD
Basic Filling 1kg Pork shoulder 1 Minced onion 150g Breadcrumbs or rusk 150ml Water 150g Diced pork fat **Seasoning** 5g Salt 25g Chopped sage 25g Chopped parsley 5g Chervil 5g Savoury **Casings** 2 metres of hog casing, soaked for at least an hour and washed inside and out.	Thoroughly mix all the dry ingredients. Finely grind the pork and mix well with the onion. Chop the pork fat into very small pieces and incorporate all the ingredients together. Fill the casings and link as required.

Tip: This sausage is another basic one which is easily amended for home experimentation.

Pork and Veal Sausage

High		
Med		
Low	Fat, Salt	

For those who do not like to cook with veal, try replacing it with duck breast. If you use chicken instead, you might need to add some fat, say 100g pork fat, finely chopped.

INGREDIENTS	METHOD
Basic Filling	Thoroughly mix the dry ingredients so that the salt, pepper and herbs are completely incorporated.
1kg Belly pork	
500g Veal	
100g Breadcrumbs or rusk	
150ml Water	Finely grind the pork. Roughly grind the veal.
Seasoning	Mix with the dry ingredients and the water.
10g Salt	
5g Black pepper	
5g Nutmeg	Stuff into casings and link as required.
5g Dried sage	
5g Mace	
Casings	
3 metres of hog casing, soaked for at least an hour and washed inside and out.	

Tip: If you use a food processor you might wish to take care with the skin.

Basic Salami Sausage

High	**Salt**	
Med		
Low		

You can add to this recipe when you are sure of making it. Do not be tempted to reduce the amount of salt. A 25g serving contains only half a gram of salt. You can flavour it with coriander, paprika, chilli, honey, tomato, onion, fennel, five-spice, anise, anything!

INGREDIENTS	METHOD
Basic Filling 500g Belly pork 500g Pork shoulder **Seasoning** 20g Salt 5g Sugar 0.5g Saltpetre (quarter of a teaspoon) 3 Crushed garlic cloves	Thoroughly mix the dry ingredients so that the salt, saltpetre, sugar and garlic are completely and uncompromisingly mixed. Roughly grind all the pork. Mix the pork with the dry ingredients and leave to marinade for at least 2 days. Stir the marinade daily, pouring off any liquid that appears.
Casings 1.5 metres of beef casing, soaked for at least 2 hours and washed inside and out.	Stuff into casings, probably enough to make 2 or 3 salamis and hang to mature around 15 Celsius, 70% relative humidity.

Tip: It will take around three to six weeks to mature the sausage. Instead of using the seasonings, think about using a commercial mix

Salmon and Dill Sausage

High		
Med		
Low	Fat, Salt	

This is almost a fishcake. You can add any number of spices in small quantities. They need to be cooked and eaten almost immediately. Fish is best ground when cold or nearly frozen.

INGREDIENTS	METHOD
Basic Filling	Skin the Salmon and make sure there are no bones.
1kg Salmon fillet (no skin)	
150g Breadcrumbs (no rusk)	Mince, probably best in a food processor, and combine all the ingredients except the water.
100ml Water	
The juice of 1 lemon	
	If the mixture is very dry, add a little of the water.
Seasoning	
5g Salt	Transfer the mix to a sheet of cling film and roll to create a rolling pin sized sausage.
5g White pepper	
	This can be poached in the cling film until cooked. Alternatively, roll small portions in breadcrumbs and fry, or stuff into sheep casings and link as required.
Casings	
None required	

Tip: You could add diced capers to this sausage.

Scarborough Fair Sausage

High	
Med	Herbs
Low	Salt

If you are going to Scarborough Fair then you might try some of these. Actually, there is no such thing as Scarborough Fair these days, and this sausage was made up—but they do taste good. It is an example of how you can take a basic recipe and make up your own.

INGREDIENTS

Basic Filling
1kg Pork shoulder
200g Breadcrumbs or rusk
200ml Water

Seasoning
10g Salt,
5g White pepper
5g Chopped parsley
10g Finely chopped sage
5g Stripped and chopped rosemary
5g Chopped thyme

Casings

2 metres of sheep casing, soaked and washed inside and out.

METHOD

Thoroughly mix the dry ingredients so that the salt and herbs are mixed with the breadcrumbs.

Finely grind the pork and mix with the dry ingredients adding the water.

Stuff into casings, and link as required.

Tip: These are good with a little garlic instead of the pepper.

Seafood Sausage

High	
Med	**Salt**
Low	

I just love the aroma of those old fashioned cockle stalls you used to get at the seaside. You can invent your own stuffing for this sausage. I use the food processor to make these because it can take some time to get the smell out of the grinder.

INGREDIENTS	METHOD
Basic Filling	Grind the crab stick to a paste.
500g Crab stick	
250g Peeled prawn	Chop the prawn and cockles into small pieces.
250g Cockles or mussels	
400g White breadcrumbs	
200ml Water	Completely mix all the ingredients and stuff into casings .
Seasoning	
15g Salt	
10g Black pepper	Link into chipolata sized sausages.
Casings	
2 metres of sheep casings, soaked and washed inside and out.	

Tip: You could try a teaspoonful of mustard, or 15g ground capers and even a dollop (say it with a French accent) of mayonnaise.

Sheftalia

High	
Med	Fat, Salt
Low	

This sausage comes from Cyprus and the reason for adding it to the list is that it uses caul fat and is placed on skewers. If you cannot get the caul (and it is becoming more difficult) simply add a beaten egg to the mix and form the sausages without it.

INGREDIENTS

METHOD

Basic Filling

1 kg Belly pork
2 Finely chopped large onions

Finely grind the pork. You might like to remove the skin, or grind it roughly at first and regrind it a second time very fine.

Seasoning

15g Salt
50g Finely chopped parsley

Combine and thoroughly mix all the ingredients.

Roll into sausage shapes and wrap in caul fat. Place onto skewers.

Casings

Half a pound of caul fat, cut into 15 cm squares.

They are great on the barbeque.

Tip: Some recipes call for a combination of pork and lamb in a ratio of 2:1 respectively. Try a little garlic too!

Shin Beef Sausage

High		
Med	**Salt**	
Low		

Beef sausages are best in small casings, slowly cooked. The addition of fat makes them more succulent, otherwise they can have a tendency to dryness.

INGREDIENTS

Basic Filling

1kg Shin beef
225g Breadcrumbs or rusk
200g Suet
250ml Water

Seasoning

15g Salt
10g Black pepper
10g Finely chopped sage
5g Powdered mustard

Casings

2 metres of sheep casing, soaked and washed inside and out.

METHOD

Thoroughly mix the dry ingredients so that the salt, pepper and herbs are completely incorporated.

Finely grind all the beef and the suet together.

Mix with the dry ingredients and the water.

Stuff into casings as required.

Tip: Try replacing the sage with very finely grated onion or chives. You can also replace the breadcrumbs with another meat.

Somerset Sausage

High	
Med	
Low	**Fat, Salt**

Somerset is famous for its apples, and so it is little wonder that these sausages incorporate apples but you can use many other fruits instead. I prefer these in thin links, so I use sheep skins.

INGREDIENTS

Basic Filling

1kg Pork shoulder
150g Breadcrumbs or rusk
200ml Dry cider
2 Bramley cooking apples
The juice of 1 lemon

Seasoning

5g Salt
5g Black pepper

Casings

2.5 metres of sheep casing, soaked and washed inside and out.

METHOD

Thoroughly mix the dry ingredients so that the salt and pepper are completely incorporated.

Peel, core and cube the apples and bring to the boil with a little water to partially cook. The lemon juice is to keep the colour.

Roughly mince the meat and the apple together.

Mix with the dry ingredients and the cider.

Stuff into casings and link as required.

Tip: You can incorporate very small pieces of peeled sweet apple into the mix.

Toulouse Sausage

High	
Med	Fat, Salt
Low	

This sausage is a basic French recipe which is reasonably low in salt and fat. It is mildly spiced with pepper and garlic and is usually cooked in a cassoulet, which is a French casserole. You can increase the amount of garlic if you like.

INGREDIENTS

Basic Filling

1kg Pork shoulder
450g Belly pork
150ml Dry white wine

Seasoning

15g Salt
10g Sugar
3 Crushed garlic cloves

Casings

2 metres of hog casing, soaked for at least an hour and washed inside and out.

METHOD

Roughly grind all the meat from the freezer to keep the fat from smearing.

Simply combine all the ingredients. Add the salt and sugar to the wine and use this to make an even mix.

Loosely stuff into hog casings and link at about a hand's length.

If you have any air pockets, prick the skin with a fine needle.

Tip: This sausage is cooked immediately prior to eating, usually boiled.

Venison and Garlic Sausage

High	
Med	Salt
Low	Fat

Venison is one of the healthiest meats you can buy, and these sausages are luxurious. The bacon adds some much needed fat because the venison is so dry, but to add too much fat would be something of a shame.

INGREDIENTS

Basic Filling

1kg Venison
500g Un-smoked fat bacon
200g Breadcrumbs or rusk
200ml Red wine

Seasoning
10g Salt
10g Black pepper
10g Sugar
15g Sage
5 Crushed garlic cloves.
5g Allspice
5g Marjoram

Casings
2 metres of hog casing, soaked for at least an hour and washed inside and out.

METHOD

Thoroughly mix the dry ingredients so that the salt, pepper and spices are completely incorporated.

Finely grind the bacon. Coarsely grind the venison.

Crush and finely mince the garlic.

Mix all the ingredients.

Stuff into casings and link as required.

Leave for 24 hours to mature.

Tip: You can add some Dijon mustard to the mix or some mustard powder.

White Pudding

High		
Med	**Salt**	
Low		

Some recipes for white pudding call for fat and skin and little else. This recipe calls for chicken and pork and is bound with breadcrumbs and milk. I was once asked how they got all the blood out of a white pudding, because they thought it was some sort of black pudding.

INGREDIENTS

Basic Filling

500g Chicken breast
500g Belly pork
300g Breadcrumbs or rusk
200ml Milk

Seasoning
20g Salt
10g White pepper
10g Mixed spice

Casings

1 metre of beef middle casing, soaked for 2 hours and washed inside and out.

METHOD

Roughly grind the pork and then grind again with the chicken to make a fine paste.

Thoroughly mix all the ingredients.

Stuff into casings and tie into two sausages with butcher's twine. This is to make sure the contents are secure.

Place in a pan of cold water and bring slowly to the boil. Simmer for 30 minutes.

Tip: Slice the cold sausage and serve with salad.

Resources

This is not an exhaustive list. There are millions of people out there to help you with sausage making. You will find there is quite a community and, whereas this book has been able to give you the basics, you will find the 'nitty gritty' of absolutely everything to do with sausage making, cooking, selling and inventing new sausages.

www.sausagemaking.org A fantastic site where you will find almost everything you will ever need to know about sausages as well as a lot more. The owner of the site, Franco, produces award winning sausage spices. You can buy equipment as well as skins and ingredients.

www.wedlinydomowe.com Information about smoking your food and there are designs for smokers you can copy.

www.sausagefans.com Packed with information, with a great recipe section.

http://home.pacbell.net/lpoli/index.htm An American site and the one to visit if you are going to make dried or smoked sausages. There are good photographs so you can compare your sausages to a master.

www.sausagelinks.co.uk One of the official trade sites. There aren't many recipes on here but lots of interesting facts.

www.thefoody.com An interesting site about food with a section about sausages which contains useful hints and recipes.

www.designasausage.com Janet and Gaynor have this great ethos about healthy cooking, and they are really enthusiastic. Here you can buy all sorts of equipment and supplies and get a load of good advice as well.

www.sausagemania.com An American site, crammed full of information. There is a fantastic, if a little bizarre, plan for a motorised stuffer grinder made from a pulley system using washing machine parts and an electric motor. (Don't try this at home!)

Sausage Equipment Suppliers (in alphabetical order).

Ascott Smallholding Supplies 0845 1306285
www.ascott.biz Everything for the smallholding. There are plenty of items for sausage makers from grinders to rusk as well as materials and items for the smallholder.

Osney Lodge Farm 01342 892216
www.sausagemaker-uk.com All kinds of meat and expertise and equipment. Training courses also available.

Sausagemaking.org 01204 433523
www.sausagemaking.org You can get almost everything you might need for sausage making through the post.

Weschenfelder   01642 247524
www.weschenfelder.co.uk This company is dedicated to sausage making and has been making skins and materials for sausages for over 80 years. They specialise in making sausage kits, amongst other things, which anyone can use, from beginners to those more advanced.

Herbs and Spices
Many of the companies above are excellent sources of pre-mixed herbs and spices for sausage making.

Continental Meat Technology. 01908 584489
www.continentalmeattechnology.co.uk Cases and spices.

Spice World 02980 675777
www.spiceworld.uk.com Almost every spice you can imagine.

Steenbergs 01765 640088
www.steenbergs.co.uk Organic spices, sausage blends and seasoning.

Butchering supplies

Catering Warehouse 0870 770 0870
www.cateringwarehouse.com Everything from refrigeration to vacuum packing machines.

Electric shop 08707 669988
www.electricshop.com Electrical kitchen equipment.

Leonards 01892 667431
www.leonards.co.uk Everything from spices to meat.

Mundial 0161 736 6868
www.mundial.uk.com Supplier of butchery knives to the industry.

Nantwich Refrigeration Services 01270 669220
www.nantwich-refrgeration.co.uk

Scobies Direct 0800 7837331
www.scobiesdirect.com Food processing equipment

The Packaging Store. 0870 751 6660
www.thepackagingstore.co.uk Everything from plastic wrap to boxes for sending sausages in the post.

Useful Contacts

Big Barn Ltd 01234 871005
www.bigbarn.co.uk Useful directory for all local producers UK wide.

Country Markets 01246 261508
www.country-markets.co.uk An association of markets with an on line buying facility.

Local Food Works 0117 9142424
www.localfoodworks.org Run by the Soil Association with aims to foster sustainable local food systems through the development of local food networks.

Meat and Livestock Commission 01908 677577
www.mlc.org.uk

The Food Standards Agency
www.food.gov.uk
Aviation House
125 Kingsway
London
WC2B 6NH

The first step for anyone wanting to sell sausages. The FSA produces guidelines on food, its safety, selling, cooking, healthy eating, food law and inspections. Useful publications include: A Guide to Food Hazards and Your Business, Food Additives, The Balanced Approach, Labelling Claims, Food Hygiene, A guide for Businesses, Starting up, Your First Steps to Running a Catering Business

The National Association of Farmers' Markets
0845 4588420
www.farmersmarkets.net

Index

Farming Books and Videos Ltd.
Publishing a wide range of titles for the farmer, smallholder and country dweller.

A Cut Above the Rest
Traditional Butchery Skills for Livestock Producers.
With David Court and Derek Newell
A comprehensive programme that covers basic butchery techniques for livestock and poultry. It includes sections on presentation, sales and marketing, sausage making, seasoning as well as step-by-step guidance on butchery.
DVD 90 mins £20

A Guide to Traditional Pig Keeping by Carol Harris
Hardback 192 pages £20

Traditional Cattle Breeds by Peter King
Hardback 128 pages £15.95

www.farmingbooksandvideos.com
Farming Books and Videos Ltd
PO Box 536
Preston
PR2 9ZY
01772 652693